38 Ways To ImplementAI Into Your Daily Life

Table of Contents:

Smart Assistants: Your Digital Companion in a Voice-Powered World

In a world that seems to move at the speed of light, finding ways to simplify our daily lives has never been more important. We often hear about the incredible advances in technology, but one innovation that's particularly transformed the way we interact with our devices is the advent of smart assistants. These digital companions, like Siri, Google Assistant, and Alexa, have become our go-to helpers in navigating the complexities of modern life.

Imagine this: you're in the middle of preparing dinner, your hands covered in flour, and you suddenly remember you need to set a timer for the roast in the oven. Instead of the usual messy struggle to dry your hands and find your phone, you simply say, "Hey Siri, set a timer for 45 minutes," and voilà! Your timer is set without missing a beat. This is just one of the countless ways smart assistants have slipped seamlessly into our daily routines, making life more convenient and efficient. The beauty of smart assistants lies in their natural language processing abilities. They understand and respond to your spoken words, creating an almost human-like interaction. This has made them invaluable in a variety of situations. Whether it's asking about the weather, getting directions, or even engaging in a casual chat, these virtual companions are always ready to lend a helping hand—or rather, a helpful voice.

But it's not just about convenience; smart assistants have evolved to offer an array of functionalities. For instance, they can send text messages for you, make phone calls, play your favorite songs, or even read you the latest news headlines. It's like having a personal assistant at your beck and call 24/7. They don't complain, they don't need a coffee break, and they certainly don't judge. Moreover, smart assistants are incredibly adaptable. They integrate seamlessly into our homes, syncing up with other smart devices like thermostats, lights, and locks. Imagine coming home on a chilly evening and simply saying, "Alexa, turn up the heat," and instantly feeling the warmth spread through your home. Or, when it's time to relax, you can say, "Hey Google, dim the lights," setting the perfect ambiance for movie night. But it's not just about home automation. These digital companions have proved their worth in helping us stay organized. Whether it's creating to-do lists, setting reminders for important meetings, or managing your calendar, they excel at keeping us on track. No more sticky notes scattered everywhere—just ask your smart assistant, and it's all neatly sorted out.
Perhaps one of the most remarkable aspects of smart assistants is their continuous learning. They adapt to

your preferences and routines, becoming more attuned to your needs over time. For instance, if you ask Alexa to play jazz music a few times, it'll remember your preference and suggest similar music in the future. It's like having a friend who knows your taste inside and out. One of the most significant advantages of smart assistants is their accessibility. They aren't confined to a single device; they're everywhere. You can access them on your smartphone, tablet, smart speakers, and even your car. This ubiquity makes them a constant presence in our lives, offering assistance wherever and whenever we need it.

Now, let's talk about the incredible potential these digital companions have in terms of accessibility. For individuals with disabilities, smart assistants are life-changing. Those with mobility impairments can control their homes with voice commands, from turning on lights to locking doors. For the visually impaired, smart assistants provide real-time information, helping them navigate the world more independently. And for those with cognitive disabilities, these virtual companions offer invaluable assistance with tasks that might otherwise be challenging.

Privacy, of course, is a concern that comes up when discussing smart assistants. After all, they're always listening to some extent, waiting for their wake word to spring into action. Companies that provide these services have invested heavily in ensuring user data is protected. It's crucial to be aware of privacy settings and to customize them to your comfort level. You have the power to determine what data is collected and how it's used.

Despite the undeniable advantages of smart assistants, they're not without their quirks and occasional misunderstandings. Sometimes, they misinterpret your words or can't quite grasp what you're asking. It can be frustrating, but it's all part of the learning curve for both users and the technology itself. Companies continuously update their algorithms to improve accuracy and responsiveness.

In conclusion, smart assistants have become an indispensable part of our lives. They simplify our daily routines, offer assistance in countless ways, and adapt to our needs like the most attentive of companions. From answering casual questions to controlling our homes and aiding those with disabilities, these virtual friends have truly changed the way we interact with technology. As they continue to evolve, it's exciting to think about the new ways they'll enhance our lives in the future. So, whether you're in the kitchen, on the road, or just lounging at home, don't hesitate to call upon your trusty smart assistant—they're always there to lend an ear, or in this case, a voice.

Smart Home Devices: Transforming Homes into Intelligent Sanctuaries

Picture this: you're on your way home after a long day at work. As you approach your house, you pull out your smartphone and, with a simple tap, you set the thermostat to the perfect temperature, turn on the lights, and even check the security cameras—all before you step inside. This isn't a scene from a sci-fi movie; it's the reality of smart home devices, the technological marvels that are transforming our homes into intelligent sanctuaries.

Smart home devices, which include gadgets like smart thermostats, lights, locks, and security systems, are at the forefront of the modern home automation movement. They're designed to enhance convenience, save energy, and provide peace of mind, and they're doing so with remarkable efficacy.

Let's start with the thermostat—the unsung hero of home comfort. Traditional thermostats required manual adjustments and offered limited scheduling options. Smart thermostats, on the other hand, are masters of efficiency. They learn your heating and cooling preferences over time and create customized schedules to maximize comfort and energy savings. Imagine walking into a cozy, perfectly heated home in the winter or a refreshingly cool oasis in the summer, all thanks to your smart thermostat's intuitive programming. But smart thermostats go beyond simple scheduling. They also offer remote control via smartphone apps or voice commands through virtual assistants like Alexa or Google Assistant. So, if you decide to stay late at the office, you can delay your heating or cooling until you're about to head home, ensuring you don't waste energy unnecessarily.

Speaking of voice commands, the integration of smart home devices with virtual assistants has revolutionized home automation. You can control your lights, locks, and more with just your voice. "Hey Alexa, turn off the lights," you say, and the room goes dark. "Ok Google, lock the front door," and your home is secure—all without lifting a finger. Lighting is another area where smart home devices shine. With smart bulbs and switches, you can set the mood in any room. Create a warm and cozy ambiance for movie night or bright, energizing light for a productive work session—all with a few taps on your smartphone. Plus, many smart lighting systems offer customizable color options, allowing you to paint your home in a spectrum of hues to suit any occasion.

But smart homes aren't just about comfort and convenience; they're also about security. Modern security systems have come a long way from the days of simple alarms. Today's smart security systems offer real-time monitoring, video surveillance, and instant alerts on your phone. You can keep an eye on your property from anywhere, receive alerts when someone approaches your front door, or even communicate with visitors through two-way audio. Moreover, some smart security systems use artificial intelligence to distinguish between normal activity and potential threats. They can tell the difference between a passing car and a suspicious person loitering around your home. This reduces false alarms and ensures you're only alerted when there's a genuine cause for concern.

The peace of mind that smart security systems provide is immeasurable. You can go on vacation and know that your home is protected. If an alarm is triggered, you'll receive an immediate notification, and you can even check the security camera footage to assess the situation remotely.

What's truly remarkable about smart home devices is their adaptability and expandability. You can start small, perhaps with a smart thermostat or a couple of smart bulbs, and gradually add more devices as your needs and budget allow. There's a vast ecosystem of compatible devices, so you can mix and match to create a home automation setup that suits your lifestyle. Another advantage is the energy savings that smart home devices bring. With smart thermostats and energy-efficient lighting, you can significantly reduce your utility bills. Smart thermostats, in particular, can pay for themselves over time with the energy savings they generate. Plus, many utility companies offer rebates and incentives for installing energy-saving devices.

However, it's not all sunshine and roses. The world of smart home devices isn't without its challenges. There are concerns about data privacy and security. With devices constantly connected to the internet, there's a risk of data breaches. It's crucial to choose reputable brands and regularly update your devices to protect your privacy. Additionally, there's a learning curve when it comes to setting up and configuring these devices. While the manufacturers have made great strides in user-friendliness, some technical know-how is often required, especially when integrating multiple devices into a cohesive system.

In conclusion, smart home devices are transforming our living spaces into intelligent sanctuaries. They offer unparalleled convenience, comfort, and security, all while helping us reduce our energy consumption. Whether you're a tech enthusiast looking to create a fully automated home or someone seeking a few simple upgrades, there's a world of possibilities waiting for you in the realm of smart home devices. As technology continues to advance, we can only imagine the incredible innovations that lie ahead, making our homes smarter, safer, and more efficient than ever before. So, as you settle into your cozy, perfectly lit living room, remember that it's not just a room; it's a smart home, and it's working tirelessly to make your life better in every way possible.

Health and Fitness Apps: Your Personalized Path to Wellness

In today's fast-paced world, maintaining a healthy lifestyle can be a challenge. Between work, family, and other responsibilities, finding the time and motivation to prioritize your health and fitness can often feel like an uphill battle. Fortunately, technology has come to the rescue in the form of health and fitness apps. These digital companions offer personalized guidance, tracking, and motivation, making it easier than ever to take control of your well-being.

The ubiquity of smartphones has put a powerful tool for health and fitness right in our pockets. Health and fitness apps cover a wide spectrum, from tracking your daily steps to providing guided workouts and even monitoring your nutrition. These apps cater to a diverse range of goals, whether you're looking to lose weight, build muscle, improve your cardiovascular fitness, or simply lead a healthier lifestyle. Let's start with the most basic yet effective feature of health and fitness apps: step tracking. Many of us carry our smartphones with us everywhere we go, and these apps can harness the built-in sensors to count our steps throughout the day. It's like having a personal pedometer, giving you instant feedback on your daily activity levels. The simple act of tracking your steps can motivate you to move more and hit your daily activity goals.

Moving up the complexity ladder, we have fitness tracking apps. These apps go beyond step counting and offer more comprehensive data on your physical activity. They can log workouts, track your heart rate, and even monitor your sleep patterns. The ability to analyze this data over time provides invaluable insights into your fitness progress and overall health. One of the standout features of fitness tracking apps is their ability to provide real-time feedback during workouts. Imagine going for a run and having a virtual coach in your ear, encouraging you to pick up the pace or maintain a steady heart rate. These apps can even suggest workout routines based on your goals and fitness level, making it easy to get started or switch up your routine.

But health and fitness apps are not just about physical activity; they also play a crucial role in nutrition tracking and meal planning. Maintaining a balanced diet is a cornerstone of a healthy lifestyle, and these apps make it easier than ever to monitor your food intake. You can log your meals, track your calorie intake, and get a breakdown of your macronutrients—all with a few taps on your smartphone. Some apps take it a step further by offering personalized meal plans and recipes tailored to your dietary preferences and goals. Whether you're a vegetarian, following a specific diet like keto or paleo, or just trying to eat more mindfully, these apps can provide you with delicious and nutritious meal ideas.

Perhaps one of the most significant advantages of health and fitness apps is their adaptability. They cater to people of all fitness levels, from beginners to seasoned athletes. You can choose your preferred workout style, whether it's yoga, strength training, HIIT, or something else entirely. The apps then adjust the intensity and duration of your workouts to match your fitness level, ensuring you get a challenging yet achievable experience. Another remarkable aspect of these apps is their community-building features. Many of them offer social components that allow you to connect with like-minded individuals, share your progress, and even participate in challenges or competitions. This sense of community can provide a powerful source of motivation and accountability, helping you stay on track with your fitness goals.

For those seeking a more holistic approach to health, mindfulness and meditation apps have gained popularity. They offer guided meditation sessions, breathing exercises, and tools to reduce stress and improve mental well-being. In a world filled with constant distractions and stressors, these apps provide a much-needed respite and a chance to reconnect with yourself.

Moreover, health and fitness apps are continuously evolving, incorporating the latest advancements in technology. Wearable fitness trackers, such as smartwatches, sync seamlessly with these apps, providing real-time data on your physical activity, heart rate, and more. This integration allows for even more accurate tracking and a deeper understanding of your health.

However, it's not all smooth sailing in the world of health and fitness apps. There are some challenges and considerations to keep in mind. First and foremost is the issue of privacy. When you use these apps, you're often sharing sensitive information about your health, activity, and eating habits. It's crucial to choose apps from reputable developers who prioritize data security and offer transparent privacy policies. Another potential pitfall is over-reliance on technology. While these apps can be incredibly helpful, they should complement, not replace, a well-rounded approach to health and fitness. It's essential to maintain a balance between technology-assisted workouts and good old-fashioned physical activity in the real world.

In conclusion, health and fitness apps have become invaluable tools for anyone looking to improve their well-being. They offer personalized guidance, track your progress, and provide motivation at your fingertips. Whether you're a fitness fanatic or just beginning your journey toward a healthier lifestyle, there's an app out there to help you reach your goals.

These apps empower you to take control of your health and fitness, providing the support and guidance you need to make lasting changes. As technology continues to advance, we can only expect these apps to become even more sophisticated and user-friendly, making it easier than ever to lead a healthy and active life. So, whether you're tracking your steps, following a guided workout, or meditating to reduce stress, know that your health and fitness app is your trusty companion on the path to wellness.

AI Navigation Apps: Your Trusted Guide to Stress-Free Travel

In a world where we're constantly on the move, navigation has become an integral part of our daily lives. Whether you're commuting to work, exploring a new city, or embarking on a road trip, finding the quickest and most efficient route is essential. Thanks to AI navigation apps like Google Maps, Waze, and Apple Maps, navigating the complexities of modern transportation has never been easier or more convenient.

Let's start by painting a common scenario. You're in an unfamiliar city, and you need to find the quickest way to reach your destination. Gone are the days of flipping through paper maps or struggling to decipher complicated public transportation schedules. With AI navigation apps, you simply open the app, type in your destination, and within seconds, you have a step-by-step route tailored to your preferences. The beauty of these apps lies in their ability to adapt to your unique needs. They provide real-time information on traffic conditions, accidents, road closures, and even speed traps, allowing you to make informed decisions about your route. No more sitting in frustrating traffic jams when you could have taken a less congested road just a few blocks away.

But AI navigation apps are not limited to road travel. They also offer options for public transportation, walking, cycling, and even ride-sharing services. This means you can rely on them whether you're driving your car, taking the subway, or simply going for a stroll in your neighborhood. Voice-guided navigation is another game-changer. Instead of constantly glancing at your phone for directions, you can focus on the road while the app provides turn-by-turn voice instructions. It's like having a knowledgeable co-pilot guiding you every step of the way.

Beyond the basics, these apps offer a slew of features that enhance your navigation experience. For instance, they can estimate your arrival time, provide alternate routes, and even suggest nearby places of interest like restaurants, gas stations, and attractions. This adds an element of spontaneity to your travels—you can easily detour for a delicious meal or an unexpected adventure without losing your way. One of the standout features of AI navigation apps is their crowd-sourced data. Waze, in particular, relies on user-generated information to provide real-time updates on road conditions. This means that as you drive, you can contribute to the community by reporting accidents, hazards, or heavy traffic. In return, you receive valuable information from other users, creating a dynamic and interconnected network of drivers helping one another.

Another area where AI navigation apps shine is in their integration with other apps and services. For instance, you can seamlessly book a ride through Uber or Lyft directly from the navigation app, eliminating the need to switch between apps. This integration extends to various other functions, such as booking restaurant reservations or finding parking spots. Moreover, these apps keep you informed about public transportation schedules and provide accurate arrival times for buses, trams, and subways. This is a lifesaver for those who rely on public transit for their daily commute, as it helps you plan your journey down to the minute.

But AI navigation apps aren't just about convenience; they also contribute to sustainability efforts by promoting efficient routes and reducing unnecessary fuel consumption. When millions of users collectively take optimal routes, it has a positive impact on the environment by lowering carbon emissions and decreasing traffic congestion. Despite their many advantages, AI navigation apps aren't without their challenges. One of the most significant concerns is privacy. These apps collect and store location data, which can be sensitive information. It's crucial to review and adjust privacy settings to ensure your data is used in a way that aligns with your comfort level. Another potential drawback is overreliance on technology. While these apps are incredibly useful, they should complement, not replace, good navigation skills. It's essential to maintain a sense of direction and map-reading ability, as technology can occasionally fail or lead you astray.

In conclusion, AI navigation apps have revolutionized the way we navigate the world. They provide real-time information, personalized routes, and a wealth of features that make travel more convenient and efficient. Whether you're commuting to work, exploring a new city, or embarking on a cross-country road trip, these apps are your trusted guide to stress-free travel.

As technology continues to advance, we can expect AI navigation apps to become even smarter and more integrated with other aspects of our lives. They will continue to play a crucial role in helping us navigate the complexities of modern transportation while making our journeys more enjoyable and efficient. So, the next time you embark on an adventure, remember to bring your trusty AI navigation app along—it's like having a personal tour guide in your pocket, ready to lead you to your destination with ease.

Transforming Your Shopping Experience: How AI Enhances Online Shopping

Online shopping has become an integral part of modern life, offering convenience, variety, and the joy of doorstep deliveries. However, the integration of

Artificial Intelligence (AI) is taking the online shopping experience to a whole new level. From personalized recommendations to streamlined customer service, AI is revolutionizing the way we shop and making our daily lives more convenient and enjoyable.

1. Personalized Product Recommendations
One of the most noticeable ways AI improves your daily online shopping experience is through personalized product recommendations. As you browse through an e-commerce platform, AI algorithms analyze your past shopping behavior, including products you've viewed, liked, or purchased. This analysis helps the AI system understand your preferences and suggests products that align with your tastes and needs.
Imagine searching for a new pair of running shoes, and suddenly, your shopping feed is flooded with various athletic footwear options, tailored to your style and activity level. AI ensures that you're not overwhelmed with irrelevant choices, making your shopping journey more efficient and enjoyable.

2. Enhanced Search and Filtering
AI-driven search functionality in online stores goes beyond simple keyword matching. AI algorithms can interpret natural language queries and provide more context-aware search results. For instance, if you're looking for a "casual summer dress," AI can understand

the attributes you're seeking and present options that fit your description.

Additionally, advanced filtering options powered by AI enable you to narrow down your choices based on size, color, price range, and other specific criteria. This helps you find the perfect product quickly and efficiently, saving you time and effort.

3. Virtual Try-On and Fitting Tools

Selecting the right size and style when shopping for clothing and accessories online can be challenging. AI has addressed this issue by introducing virtual try-on and fitting tools. Using augmented reality (AR), these tools allow you to see how clothing and accessories would look on you without needing to try them on physically. For example, if you're shopping for eyeglasses, you can use an AI-powered virtual try-on tool to see how different frames would look on your face. This feature reduces the uncertainty of online shopping and increases your confidence in making the right choice.

4. Price Comparison and Alerts

AI helps you find the best deals and save money while shopping online. Price comparison websites and browser extensions powered by AI can analyze prices from multiple retailers and display the best options for the product you're interested in.

Additionally, AI-driven price tracking tools can notify you when the price of an item you're eyeing drops or falls within your budget. This ensures that you get the best possible deal on your desired products.

5. Chatbots for Instant Customer Support
Customer service is a critical aspect of online shopping, and AI-powered chatbots are transforming how you get assistance. These virtual assistants are available 24/7 to answer your questions, provide information about products, and assist with various inquiries.
Chatbots can offer quick responses and handle routine tasks such as order tracking, returns, and refunds, freeing up human customer service agents to focus on more complex issues. This means you can get the assistance you need at any time, without waiting in long phone queues or dealing with delayed email responses.

6. Streamlined Checkout and Payment
AI streamlines the checkout process, making it faster and more convenient. Features like one-click checkout and autofill for payment and shipping information are made possible through AI. These features reduce the time and effort required to complete a purchase, enhancing your shopping experience.
Moreover, AI-driven fraud detection algorithms work in the background to ensure the security of your

transactions. They analyze patterns and behaviors to detect and prevent fraudulent
activities, protecting your financial information.

7. Dynamic Pricing and Discounts
AI algorithms also play a role in dynamic pricing and discounts. Online retailers can adjust prices in real-time based on factors such as demand, supply, and user behavior. This means that the price you see for a product may change over time.
Furthermore, AI can analyze your shopping history and offer personalized discounts and promotions. If you frequently purchase a particular brand or type of product, the AI system may provide you with exclusive offers tailored to your preferences.

8. Efficient Inventory Management
AI helps retailers manage their inventory more efficiently, ensuring that popular products remain in stock and reducing the chances of items being out of stock. Machine learning algorithms analyze historical sales data, demand fluctuations, and seasonality patterns to optimize inventory levels.
This means you're more likely to find the products you want in stock, preventing disappointment and the need to wait for restocking.

9. Recommendations for Complementary Products

In addition to suggesting products you might like, AI also recommends complementary items that go well with your selected products. For instance, if you're buying a camera, AI might suggest accessories like lenses, tripods, or camera bags.
These recommendations enhance your shopping experience by helping you discover items that can enhance the utility or enjoyment of your purchases.

10. Eco-Friendly Shopping
AI is also contributing to eco-friendly shopping by providing information about the sustainability of products. Some online retailers now include sustainability scores or labels on their products, indicating their environmental impact.
AI algorithms analyze factors such as materials, production methods, and transportation to determine a product's sustainability score. This enables you to make more environmentally conscious choices when shopping online.

In conclusion, AI has brought a wave of innovation and convenience to online shopping, making it a more personalized, efficient, and enjoyable experience. From personalized recommendations to virtual try-ons and chatbot support, AI-driven tools and technologies enhance every aspect of your shopping journey. As AI continues to advance, we can expect even more innovations that will redefine the way we shop online, creating a future where convenience, personalization, and efficiency are the norms of online retail therapy.

AI-Powered News and Content Curation: Enhancing Your Daily Life

In our fast-paced digital age, staying informed and engaged with the world has never been easier, thanks to Artificial Intelligence (AI) in the realm of news and content curation. AI is revolutionizing the way we consume information, providing us with personalized, relevant, and timely news, articles, and content tailored to our interests and preferences. Here's how AI is enhancing your daily life through news and content curation:

1. Personalized News Feeds
One of the most noticeable ways AI is improving your daily life is through personalized news feeds. AI algorithms analyze your reading habits, search history, and interactions with content to curate a news feed tailored to your interests. This means you're more likely to see articles and news stories that align with your preferences and concerns.

Imagine waking up and opening your news app to find a feed filled with articles on topics that genuinely matter to you, whether it's technology, sports, health, or politics. AI ensures that you're not bombarded with irrelevant or uninteresting news, making your daily information intake more engaging and efficient.

2. Real-time Updates

AI-powered news apps and websites provide real-time updates on breaking news and events. These platforms use natural language processing and machine learning algorithms to scan news sources, social media, and other online content for the latest information.

This means you can stay informed about important developments as they happen, whether it's a major political event, a natural disaster, or a sports championship. AI ensures that you're always in the know and can react promptly to relevant news.

3. Diverse Perspectives

AI in news curation is not limited to echo chambers; it aims to provide diverse perspectives. Algorithms take into account your interests while also introducing you to articles and viewpoints from different sources and ideologies.

This ensures that you get a well-rounded view of current events and issues, helping you form informed opinions and engage in thoughtful discussions. AI encourages open-mindedness and critical thinking by exposing you to a variety of perspectives.

4. Contextual Content Recommendations
AI doesn't stop at news articles; it extends to recommending relevant content across various media formats. For instance, if you read a news article about a space mission, AI algorithms may recommend related content, such as podcasts, videos, or documentaries on space exploration.
This contextual content recommendation enriches your daily life by providing a multimedia learning experience that goes beyond text-based news.

5. Fact-Checking and Verification
Misinformation and fake news are prevalent in today's digital landscape, but AI is working to combat this issue. AI-driven fact-checking tools analyze the credibility of news sources and flag potentially false or misleading information.
These tools can help you make more informed decisions about the news you consume, ensuring that you rely on accurate and trustworthy sources for your daily information.

6. Time Efficiency
AI saves you time by summarizing lengthy articles and news stories. AI-driven algorithms can generate concise

summaries that capture the key points of an article, allowing you to grasp the main ideas without investing a significant amount of time.

This time efficiency is particularly valuable in today's busy world, where multitasking and quick information consumption are the norms.

7. Accessibility Features

AI-powered news and content curation platforms are also making strides in accessibility. Text-to-speech technologies enable individuals with visual impairments to consume news articles and content through audio. Moreover, AI-driven transcription services can convert spoken content, such as podcasts or video content, into text, making it accessible to individuals who prefer reading or have hearing impairments.

8. Content Moderation and Filter Bubbles

AI is working to address concerns about content moderation and filter bubbles. AI algorithms can detect and flag inappropriate or harmful content, helping to maintain a safe and respectful online environment. Additionally, AI can identify when you're stuck in a filter bubble, where you're only exposed to content that aligns with your existing beliefs. It can then introduce you to content from diverse viewpoints, encouraging a more balanced and open perspective.

9. Multilingual News and Translation

In an increasingly globalized world, AI-powered translation services are breaking down language barriers. AI algorithms can translate news articles and content from different languages into your preferred language, allowing you to access a wealth of information from around the world.

This enhances your daily life by expanding your horizons and providing insights from diverse cultural perspectives.

10. Personalized Learning

AI-driven content curation isn't limited to news; it extends to educational content as well. Whether you're interested in learning a new language, improving your cooking skills, or exploring a new hobby, AI can curate educational content tailored to your goals and preferences.

Imagine receiving daily lessons, tips, and tutorials that align with your interests and learning style, making your journey of continuous learning more engaging and accessible.

While AI has transformed the way we consume news and content, it's important to approach these advancements with critical thinking and media literacy. It's essential to be aware of potential biases in algorithms and verify information from multiple sources, especially when dealing with controversial or sensitive topics.

In conclusion, AI-powered news and content curation are enriching our daily lives by providing personalized, real-time, and diverse information experiences. From personalized news feeds and fact-checking to content recommendations and accessibility features, AI ensures that you stay informed, engaged, and open-minded in our fast-paced digital age. As AI continues to advance, the future of news and content consumption promises to be even more tailored and informative, enhancing our daily lives in ways we have yet to fully imagine.

Streamlining Your Inbox: How AI Enhances Email Filtering for a Better Daily Life

Email has become an indispensable part of our daily lives, serving as a primary means of communication for personal and professional purposes. However, the sheer volume of emails we receive can be overwhelming, leading to email fatigue and decreased productivity. Fortunately, Artificial Intelligence (AI) has stepped in to revolutionize email filtering, making our lives easier and more efficient. Here's how AI is transforming email filtering to improve your daily life:

1. Spam Filtering

One of the most noticeable ways AI improves your daily life is through spam filtering. AI-powered email providers employ sophisticated algorithms that can accurately identify and divert spam emails away from your primary inbox.

AI analyzes various factors, including email content, sender reputation, and user feedback, to determine whether an email is spam. This ensures that you're not inundated with unwanted advertisements, phishing attempts, or irrelevant messages, allowing you to focus on important emails.

2. Inbox Organization

AI goes beyond simple spam filtering; it helps organize your inbox effectively. By categorizing emails into folders or labels, AI ensures that you can quickly locate and prioritize emails based on their content.

For example, AI can automatically categorize emails as "Social," "Promotions," "Updates," or "Primary." This organization helps you manage your inbox efficiently, preventing important emails from getting buried under a deluge of less critical messages.

3. Smart Suggestions

AI-driven email platforms provide smart suggestions for organizing your inbox. These suggestions may include archiving, deleting, or moving emails to specific folders. AI algorithms analyze your email behavior and suggest actions that align with your preferences.

This feature streamlines your daily email management, reducing the time spent on mundane tasks and enabling you to focus on more critical matters.

4. Priority Inbox

AI helps identify emails that are most likely to be important to you. By analyzing your interaction history, AI can flag emails from senders you frequently correspond with or categorize emails that contain keywords or phrases indicative of urgency.

This prioritization ensures that you don't miss critical emails amidst the noise of your inbox, enhancing your daily efficiency and responsiveness.

5. Automated Responses

AI-driven email platforms offer automated response suggestions. These suggestions are based on the content and context of the email you've received. For example, if you receive a meeting invitation, AI may suggest responses like "Accept," "Decline," or "Propose a different time."

This feature simplifies your email communication, allowing you to respond promptly and professionally without the need to compose detailed messages for routine requests.

6. Email Summaries

AI can generate daily or weekly email summaries that highlight the most critical messages and updates. These summaries provide a concise overview of your inbox, helping you stay informed without sifting through numerous emails.

By condensing your email activity into a digestible format, AI enhances your daily life by saving you time and reducing email-related stress.

7. Advanced Search and Filtering

AI improves your email search capabilities significantly. Advanced search and filtering options powered by AI allow you to find specific emails, attachments, or conversations quickly.

For instance, you can search for emails from a particular sender within a specific date range or find attachments containing specific keywords. This feature enhances your daily productivity by minimizing the time spent searching for critical information buried in your inbox.

8. Language Translation

In an increasingly globalized world, AI-driven email platforms offer language translation services. These services can automatically translate emails received in foreign languages into your preferred language, ensuring you can understand and respond to international communications without language barriers.

This feature opens up opportunities for global collaboration and expands your daily communication horizons.

9. Attachment Handling

AI-powered email platforms can analyze email attachments for potential security risks. They can detect malicious files or phishing attempts, helping protect you from email-based threats.

Moreover, AI can assist in organizing and managing attachments. It can suggest categorizing attachments based on file type or relevance, ensuring you have easy access to important documents when you need them.

10. Sentiment Analysis

AI can analyze the sentiment of incoming emails, providing insights into the emotional tone of the message. This can be particularly useful for professionals who need to gauge the sentiment of customer feedback, assess the tone of client communications, or identify potential issues in team correspondence.

By flagging emails with specific sentiments, AI enables you to address emotional or critical emails promptly and effectively.

While AI has revolutionized email filtering and management, it's important to use these tools mindfully. Be aware of privacy considerations and ensure that you're comfortable with the level of access AI-driven email providers have to your data. Additionally, continue to exercise critical thinking and judgment when assessing email content, especially in situations where security or sensitive information is involved.

In conclusion, AI-powered email filtering has significantly improved our daily lives by reducing email clutter, enhancing organization, and simplifying communication. From spam filtering to advanced search capabilities and sentiment analysis, AI ensures that your email experience is efficient, streamlined, and productive. As AI continues to advance, the future of email filtering holds the promise of even more personalized and intelligent features, making our daily communication more seamless and enjoyable.

Breaking Language Barriers: How AI Enhances Language Translation for Your Daily Life

In our interconnected world, language is a powerful tool for communication, understanding, and collaboration.

However, linguistic diversity can sometimes be a barrier to effective communication. Fortunately, Artificial Intelligence (AI) has stepped in to break down these language barriers by revolutionizing language translation. From travel to business and everyday interactions, AI-driven language translation is significantly improving our daily lives. Here's how:

1. Seamless Travel Experiences
Traveling to a foreign country can be an exciting adventure, but it can also be challenging when you don't speak the local language. AI-powered language translation apps and devices are making travel more accessible and enjoyable.
Imagine strolling through the bustling streets of Tokyo and using your smartphone to instantly translate street signs, menus, and conversations. AI translation apps can provide real-time translations of written and spoken text, helping you navigate foreign environments with ease.

2. Multilingual Business Communication
In today's globalized business world, multilingual communication is essential. AI-powered translation tools enable businesses to engage with international partners, clients, and customers in their native languages.
These tools can automatically translate emails, documents, and website content, ensuring that your business messages are clear and culturally sensitive. This

capability fosters stronger relationships and enhances your daily business operations.

3. Education and Learning Opportunities
AI-driven language translation is a game-changer for language learners. Language learning apps and platforms use AI to provide real-time translations, helping learners understand and practice in a foreign language.
For example, if you're learning Spanish, AI can translate English sentences into Spanish, allowing you to compare your answers and improve your language skills. This interactive approach to language learning makes it more engaging and accessible.

4. Access to Global Content
AI-driven translation is expanding access to global content. With the help of AI, you can enjoy books, articles, videos, and news from around the world in your native language.
Online content, such as news articles, blogs, and YouTube videos, can be instantly translated into your preferred language, broadening your horizons and exposing you to diverse perspectives and cultures.

5. Enhanced Cross-Cultural Communication
In multicultural and diverse societies, AI translation fosters cross-cultural understanding and inclusion. AI-

driven translation tools enable individuals from different linguistic backgrounds to communicate seamlessly.
For instance, in a diverse workplace, employees can use AI-powered translation apps to converse with colleagues who speak different languages. This inclusivity enhances teamwork and collaboration, making the workplace more harmonious and productive.

6. Language Accessibility in Customer Service
AI-driven translation is also improving customer service. Chatbots and virtual assistants equipped with translation capabilities can assist customers in their preferred languages, regardless of the company's location.
This ensures that customers receive support and information in a language they are comfortable with, resulting in higher customer satisfaction and loyalty.

7. Enhanced Global Collaboration
AI translation plays a pivotal role in global collaboration. In research, academia, and international projects, language translation tools break down communication barriers among experts and collaborators from different countries.
Teams can collaborate on projects, share research findings, and participate in international conferences without the hindrance of language barriers. This fosters innovation and advances knowledge sharing.

8. Emergency Communication

In emergency situations, communication is crucial, especially in regions with diverse languages. AI-powered translation devices and apps can bridge the communication gap between emergency responders and individuals who speak different languages.

This ensures that vital information and instructions are accurately conveyed during critical moments, enhancing safety and saving lives.

9. Preservation of Indigenous Languages

AI-driven language translation has a role in preserving endangered and indigenous languages. These languages often face the risk of extinction due to limited speakers and documentation.

Translation tools can help document, transcribe, and translate indigenous languages, making it easier to pass down cultural heritage and knowledge to future generations.

10. Accessible Healthcare Information

Access to healthcare information is a basic right, and AI-driven translation ensures that healthcare resources are accessible to all. Medical websites, instructions, and health apps can provide translations in multiple languages, ensuring that individuals can access important health information. This accessibility promotes better health outcomes and enables people to make informed decisions about their well-being.

While AI-powered translation has significantly improved our daily lives, it's important to remember that it's not without challenges. Machine translation can sometimes produce inaccuracies or lack cultural nuances. It's essential to use AI translation as a tool for communication but be mindful of its limitations, especially in contexts that require precise, context-rich translations.

In conclusion, AI-driven language translation is a transformative force that enhances our daily lives in numerous ways, from seamless travel experiences to improved cross-cultural communication and access to global content. As AI technology continues to advance, the future of language translation holds the promise of even more accurate, culturally sensitive, and accessible communication across languages and cultures. By breaking down language barriers, AI is helping us build a more interconnected and inclusive world.

Elevating Your Fitness Journey: How AI-Powered Virtual Personal Trainers Enhance Your Daily Life

Maintaining a healthy lifestyle and achieving fitness goals can be a challenging endeavor, especially when it comes to staying motivated and having access to professional guidance. However, the integration of Artificial Intelligence (AI) into fitness has ushered in a new era of personalized and accessible training. AI-powered virtual personal trainers are revolutionizing the way we approach fitness and are significantly improving our daily lives. Here's how:

1. Personalized Workout Plans
One of the most prominent ways AI enhances your daily life is by providing personalized workout plans. AI algorithms analyze your fitness goals, current fitness level, and any health constraints you may have to create tailored workout routines that align with your objectives. Imagine having a virtual personal trainer who designs workouts specifically for you, taking into account your preferences, whether you prefer strength training, cardio, or flexibility exercises. These personalized plans make it easier to stay motivated and see real progress in your fitness journey.

2. Real-Time Feedback and Corrections

AI-powered virtual trainers provide real-time feedback during your workouts. Through wearable devices or smartphone apps, these trainers can monitor your form and technique, offering instant corrections to help you perform exercises safely and effectively.

This real-time guidance reduces the risk of injuries and ensures that you're getting the most out of your workouts, enhancing the overall quality of your fitness routine.

3. Adaptation to Your Progress

AI doesn't just provide static workout plans; it adapts to your progress. As you advance in your fitness journey, AI algorithms continually adjust your workouts to challenge you appropriately.

Whether you're aiming to increase the weight you lift, improve your running pace, or enhance your endurance, AI ensures that your workouts evolve to match your capabilities, helping you reach your goals more efficiently.

4. Access to Expertise Anytime, Anywhere

One of the key advantages of AI-powered virtual personal trainers is the ability to access expert guidance anytime and anywhere. Whether you're at the gym, at home, or on the road, your virtual trainer is with you.

This flexibility eliminates the need for in-person training sessions and allows you to maintain your fitness routine even when your schedule is busy, enhancing your daily life by making fitness more accessible and convenient.

5. Nutritional Guidance
AI-powered fitness apps often include nutritional guidance. They can analyze your dietary habits, track your calorie intake, and provide personalized meal recommendations based on your fitness goals.
This holistic approach to health and fitness ensures that you're not only working out effectively but also fueling your body optimally, contributing to overall well-being and energy levels in your daily life.

6. Motivation and Accountability
Staying motivated is a common challenge in fitness. AI-powered virtual trainers act as motivational partners by setting goals, tracking your progress, and sending reminders for your workouts.
They can even gamify your fitness experience by awarding badges or rewards for achieving milestones, turning your fitness routine into an engaging and fun daily activity.

7. Mental Health and Stress Management
AI isn't limited to physical fitness; it also addresses mental health and stress management. Virtual trainers

often include mindfulness and meditation exercises to help you manage stress and improve your mental well-being.
These features contribute to a more balanced and relaxed daily life, helping you cope with the pressures of work, life, and personal challenges.

8. Injury Prevention
AI analyzes your exercise history and can identify patterns that may increase your risk of injury. Virtual trainers can provide recommendations to prevent overtraining and suggest recovery strategies.
This proactive approach to injury prevention ensures that you can maintain a consistent fitness routine without interruptions due to injuries.

9. Community and Social Support
Many AI-powered fitness platforms offer community features that connect you with like-minded individuals and fitness enthusiasts. You can join groups, participate in challenges, and share your progress with others.
This sense of community and social support not only motivates you but also enhances your daily life by creating connections with people who share your fitness goals and interests.

10. Data-Driven Insights

AI collects and analyzes a vast amount of data about your fitness habits, including your workout frequency, sleep patterns, and overall health. It can provide valuable insights into your fitness journey, helping you make informed decisions about your goals and strategies. By tracking your progress over time, AI ensures that your fitness routine is efficient and effective, contributing to a healthier and more active daily life.

While AI-powered virtual personal trainers offer numerous benefits, it's important to approach fitness technology with mindfulness. It's essential to balance virtual training with self-awareness and listen to your body. AI can provide guidance, but it's important to be attuned to your physical sensations and any signs of discomfort or overexertion.

In conclusion, AI-powered virtual personal trainers are transforming the way we approach fitness, making it more personalized, accessible, and motivating. By providing tailored workout plans, real-time feedback, and adaptable routines, AI is helping individuals achieve their fitness goals and live healthier, more active daily lives. As AI continues to advance, the future of fitness holds the promise of even more innovative and integrated solutions, ensuring that fitness remains an integral part of our well-rounded and fulfilling lifestyles.

Nurturing Mental Wellness: How AI-Enhanced Mental Health Apps Transform Your Daily Life

In today's fast-paced and often stressful world, maintaining mental wellness is a crucial aspect of our overall health. Fortunately, the integration of Artificial Intelligence (AI) into mental health apps is revolutionizing the way we approach self-care and emotional well-being. AI-powered mental health apps are significantly improving our daily lives by providing accessible, personalized, and effective tools for managing mental health. Here's how:

1. Personalized Self-Help
One of the most remarkable ways AI enhances your daily life is by offering personalized self-help resources. These apps use AI algorithms to assess your mental health, including your stress levels, mood fluctuations, and sleep patterns.
Imagine having a mental health companion that tailors self-help strategies based on your individual needs. Whether you're struggling with anxiety, depression, or everyday stress, AI helps you access resources and coping mechanisms that resonate with your unique circumstances.

2. 24/7 Support

AI-powered mental health apps provide 24/7 support. They are always available to listen, provide guidance, and offer assistance, even when human support might not be readily accessible.

This continuous support ensures that you have a mental health companion whenever you need one, contributing to your daily life by offering a sense of security and emotional stability.

3. Mood Tracking and Analysis

AI apps track and analyze your mood over time. By regularly recording your feelings and emotional states, these apps can identify patterns and potential triggers. This self-awareness contributes to your daily life by helping you recognize patterns in your emotional well-being, making it easier to take proactive steps to manage your mental health effectively.

4. Cognitive Behavioral Therapy (CBT) Tools

Cognitive Behavioral Therapy (CBT) is a well-established therapeutic approach for managing various mental health conditions. AI-powered mental health apps often incorporate CBT techniques and exercises.

Imagine having access to interactive CBT tools on your smartphone. These tools guide you through cognitive restructuring, relaxation techniques, and exposure therapy, empowering you to actively manage and improve your mental health.

5. Medication Reminders
For individuals on medication for mental health conditions, AI apps offer medication reminders and tracking features. They ensure that you adhere to your medication schedule, promoting better treatment outcomes.
By incorporating medication management into your daily routine, AI helps you take charge of your mental health and ensures that you're receiving the full benefits of your treatment.

6. Anonymous Support Communities
AI-powered mental health apps often feature anonymous support communities where individuals can connect with others facing similar challenges. These communities provide a safe and empathetic space to share experiences, seek advice, and offer support.
Being part of such a community fosters a sense of belonging and reduces feelings of isolation, enhancing your daily life by providing a support system that understands your struggles.

7. Immediate Crisis Intervention
AI is equipped to identify signs of crisis and intervene immediately. If the app detects severe distress or the risk

of self-harm, it can provide emergency resources and connect you with crisis helplines.

This life-saving feature ensures that you have access to immediate assistance during moments of crisis, emphasizing your safety and well-being in your daily life.

8. Sleep Improvement

Mental health and sleep are closely intertwined. AI apps can track your sleep patterns and offer strategies to improve sleep quality.

Imagine receiving personalized sleep recommendations that help you establish healthy sleep routines, address insomnia, and wake up feeling refreshed, contributing to your daily life by enhancing your overall well-being and mental clarity.

9. Progress Tracking

AI-powered apps enable you to track your mental health progress over time. They provide visualizations and insights into your emotional well-being, such as improvements in mood, reduced stress levels, or increased resilience.

Tracking your progress reinforces a sense of achievement and motivates you to continue your mental health journey, making daily life more fulfilling and hopeful.

10. Privacy and Confidentiality

AI-driven mental health apps prioritize privacy and confidentiality. They often use advanced encryption and security measures to protect your sensitive information. Knowing that your mental health data is secure and private allows you to use these apps with confidence, ensuring that you can focus on self-care without concerns about data breaches or privacy breaches. While AI-powered mental health apps offer numerous benefits, it's essential to use them as a supplement to, rather than a replacement for, professional mental health care. These apps are valuable tools for self-care and early intervention, but they should not substitute for the expertise of mental health professionals when needed.

In conclusion, AI-enhanced mental health apps are revolutionizing the way we prioritize and manage our emotional well-being. By providing personalized support, self-help resources, and continuous assistance, AI empowers individuals to take an active role in their mental health journey, ultimately enhancing their daily lives. As AI continues to advance, the future of mental health apps holds the promise of even more innovative, effective, and accessible solutions that promote mental wellness and emotional resilience in our increasingly complex world.

Sunny Days Ahead: How AI-Enhanced Weather Forecasts Transform Your Daily Life

Weather plays a pivotal role in our daily lives, influencing our plans, routines, and overall well-being. Accurate weather forecasts help us make informed decisions and stay prepared for whatever Mother Nature has in store. The integration of Artificial Intelligence (AI) into weather forecasting is revolutionizing the way we access and utilize weather information, significantly improving our daily lives. Here's how:

1. Hyper-Precision Forecasting
One of the most noticeable ways AI improves your daily life is through hyper-precision forecasting. Traditional weather models rely on large-scale data, but AI algorithms can process vast amounts of data from various sources, including satellites, weather stations, and even smartphones.
Imagine receiving a weather forecast that predicts rain within a few minutes in your exact location rather than a general prediction for your city. AI-powered weather forecasts provide precise and location-specific information, ensuring you're prepared for sudden changes in weather conditions.

2. Real-Time Updates

AI-driven weather apps provide real-time updates, keeping you informed about changing weather patterns throughout the day. These apps use radar and satellite imagery to track storms, temperature fluctuations, and precipitation.

Whether you're planning a picnic, a hike, or a road trip, AI ensures that you receive timely updates, allowing you to adjust your plans and stay safe.

3. Improved Severe Weather Alerts

Severe weather events like hurricanes, tornadoes, and floods can have a significant impact on our daily lives. AI-enhanced weather forecasts excel in predicting and tracking such events with precision.

These forecasts provide early warnings and alerts, helping you take necessary precautions, evacuate if required, and protect your family and property during extreme weather conditions.

4. Traffic and Commute Planning

Weather conditions can significantly affect traffic and commute times. AI-powered weather apps integrate with navigation systems to provide real-time weather-related traffic updates.

Imagine receiving a notification that suggests an alternate route to avoid heavy rain or snow. AI helps you plan your commute more efficiently, reducing stress and delays in your daily routine.

5. Agricultural Planning

For farmers and agricultural communities, weather forecasts are vital for crop planning and management. AI-enhanced weather forecasts provide accurate data on rainfall, temperature, and humidity, helping farmers optimize planting and harvesting schedules.
This technology contributes to food security and agricultural sustainability, which has a far-reaching impact on society's daily lives.

6. Energy Efficiency

AI-driven weather forecasts contribute to energy efficiency by helping consumers and energy providers manage their energy consumption more effectively. For instance, AI can predict extreme temperature fluctuations, allowing homeowners to adjust their thermostat settings and save on heating and cooling costs. Energy providers can also optimize energy production based on weather forecasts, ensuring a stable supply.

7. Outdoor Activity Planning

Whether you're planning a family picnic, a camping trip, or a day at the beach, AI-enhanced weather forecasts make outdoor activity planning more convenient.

These forecasts provide not only the expected weather conditions but also insights into UV index, pollen levels, and air quality, helping you plan activities that are safe and enjoyable for your family and friends.

8. Improved Disaster Preparedness
In regions prone to natural disasters, AI-powered weather forecasts are indispensable for disaster preparedness and response. These forecasts provide early warnings and enable governments and relief organizations to mobilize resources and provide assistance.
This technology enhances your daily life by ensuring that you and your community are better equipped to cope with natural disasters and their aftermath.

9. Air Travel Safety
For frequent flyers, AI-enhanced weather forecasts are a game-changer. These forecasts provide detailed information about weather conditions at departure and arrival airports, as well as along flight routes.
This information helps airlines make informed decisions about flight delays, diversions, and cancellations, ensuring passenger safety and reducing travel disruptions.

10. Eco-Friendly Living

AI-powered weather forecasts also support eco-friendly living. They provide information on renewable energy generation, such as wind and solar power, helping individuals and businesses harness clean energy sources more efficiently. By promoting sustainable practices, AI contributes to a greener and more environmentally conscious daily life.

While AI-enhanced weather forecasting offers numerous benefits, it's important to use these forecasts alongside critical thinking and judgment. Weather can be unpredictable, and even the most advanced AI models have limitations. It's wise to consider multiple sources of weather information, especially for critical decisions.

In conclusion, AI-enhanced weather forecasts are transforming the way we interact with and adapt to our ever-changing environment. By providing hyper-precision, real-time updates, and improved alerts for severe weather events, AI contributes to safety, convenience, and well-being in our daily lives. As AI technology continues to advance, the future of weather forecasting promises even more accurate and insightful predictions, ensuring that we're always prepared for whatever weather comes our way.

Summarizing the Advantages: How AI-Enhanced Text Summarization Improves Your Daily Life

In today's information-rich world, we encounter an overwhelming amount of text every day. Whether it's news articles, research papers, emails, or online content, the ability to quickly grasp the essential information is invaluable. This is where Artificial Intelligence (AI) comes into play, offering text summarization tools that significantly enhance our daily lives. Here's how AI-Enhanced Text Summarization is making a difference:

1. Time Efficiency

One of the most noticeable ways AI improves your daily life is by saving you time. AI-driven text summarization tools can analyze lengthy documents, articles, or reports and provide concise summaries within seconds.
Imagine having to sift through a 10,000-word research paper for a key piece of information versus receiving a well-structured summary that captures the main points in just a few paragraphs. AI ensures that you can quickly access the core ideas without investing excessive time in reading lengthy texts.

2. Enhanced Information Retrieval

AI text summarization significantly enhances your ability to retrieve information quickly and effectively. Whether you're a student, a professional, or someone seeking knowledge, the ability to access summarized information streamlines your research and information gathering process.

By providing succinct summaries of articles, books, or documents, AI ensures that you can find relevant information promptly, improving your productivity and knowledge acquisition.

3. Improved Decision-Making

In a professional context, making informed decisions is crucial. AI-enhanced text summarization tools empower you to make well-informed choices by providing concise overviews of complex documents and reports.

Imagine being a manager responsible for evaluating multiple project proposals. AI can summarize each proposal, highlighting key details, strengths, and weaknesses, enabling you to make informed decisions efficiently.

4. Enhanced Learning

For students and lifelong learners, AI-driven text summarization enhances the learning experience. Whether you're studying for exams, researching a topic, or exploring a new subject, AI can condense large

volumes of information into manageable, digestible summaries.
This capability simplifies the learning process, ensuring that you understand and retain critical concepts while saving time.

5. Multilingual Summaries

AI-driven text summarization isn't limited to a single language. These tools can summarize text in multiple languages, making information accessible to a global audience.
This feature is particularly valuable in an increasingly interconnected world where individuals seek information from diverse cultural and linguistic sources.

6. Content Curation

AI-driven content curation platforms use text summarization to deliver relevant and engaging content. These platforms analyze articles, blog posts, and news stories, summarizing them to provide users with a curated feed of concise and insightful information. Imagine opening a news app that delivers summaries of the day's top stories tailored to your interests. AI ensures that you stay informed without overwhelming you with information overload.

7. Accessibility

Text summarization tools enhance accessibility for individuals with disabilities. They can summarize text content and convert it into audio formats, making it accessible to people with visual impairments or those who prefer audio content.

This accessibility feature ensures that everyone has equal access to information and knowledge, promoting inclusivity in daily life.

8. Content Moderation

AI text summarization tools are also used for content moderation on digital platforms. They can summarize user-generated content, such as comments or reviews, to detect and flag inappropriate or harmful content.

This ensures a safer and more respectful online environment, protecting users from harmful experiences.

9. Legal and Compliance

In legal and regulatory fields, AI-driven text summarization tools help professionals stay up-to-date with complex and ever-changing laws and regulations. These tools can summarize legal documents, helping legal practitioners quickly identify critical details and changes.

This streamlines legal research and ensures that professionals remain compliant with the latest legal requirements.

10. Customization

AI allows for customization in text summarization. Users can adjust parameters to tailor summaries to their preferences. For instance, you can choose to receive summaries that emphasize different aspects of a text, such as key statistics, main ideas, or critical arguments. This customization ensures that the summaries align with your specific needs and priorities.

While AI-enhanced text summarization offers numerous advantages, it's important to remember that these tools are not infallible. They rely on algorithms, and there can be limitations in understanding context, nuance, or the human element in text.

In conclusion, AI-enhanced text summarization is a transformative force that significantly improves our daily lives. By providing time-efficient, informative, and accessible summaries, AI ensures that we can navigate the information landscape more effectively, whether we're making decisions, learning, staying informed, or curating content. As AI technology continues to advance, the future of text summarization holds the promise of even more intelligent and context-aware tools, further enhancing our daily experience in an information-rich world.

Unleashing Creativity: How AI-Powered Content Creation Elevates Your Daily Life

Content creation has become an integral part of our daily lives. Whether you're a blogger, a social media enthusiast, a marketer, or simply someone who enjoys expressing their thoughts, Artificial Intelligence (AI) is revolutionizing the way we produce content. AI-powered content creation tools are significantly improving our daily lives by enhancing creativity, productivity, and accessibility. Here's how:

1. Automated Content Generation
One of the most noticeable ways AI enhances your daily life is by automating content generation. AI-powered tools can generate written content, including articles, blog posts, product descriptions, and more.
Imagine having an AI writing assistant that can quickly create high-quality content on a wide range of topics. This not only saves you time but also ensures that you consistently produce engaging and informative content.

2. Content Personalization
AI-driven content creation tools can personalize content for specific audiences. These tools analyze user data and

preferences to tailor content, ensuring that it resonates with your target audience.

For instance, if you're running an e-commerce website, AI can create product recommendations and personalized shopping guides based on individual user behaviors and preferences.

3. Multilingual Content Creation

AI breaks down language barriers by enabling multilingual content creation. These tools can translate and adapt content into different languages, making it accessible to a global audience.

This feature is invaluable in an interconnected world, allowing individuals and businesses to reach a wider and more diverse audience.

4. Video and Visual Content

AI is not limited to text-based content creation; it's also transforming video and visual content. AI-driven tools can generate video scripts, produce animations, and even create visual designs and artwork.

For content creators on platforms like YouTube and Instagram, AI tools provide new creative possibilities, simplifying the production of engaging multimedia content.

5. Content Suggestion and Idea Generation

Writer's block is a common challenge for content creators. AI can provide content suggestions and generate creative ideas based on trending topics, user interests, and historical data.
Having an AI brainstorming partner ensures that you always have fresh and engaging ideas for your blog, social media posts, or marketing campaigns.

6. Enhanced Editing and Proofreading

AI-powered content creation tools offer advanced editing and proofreading capabilities. They can identify grammatical errors, style inconsistencies, and readability issues.
Whether you're a student working on an essay, a professional crafting a report, or a blogger perfecting your posts, AI ensures that your content is error-free and polished.

7. SEO Optimization

AI-driven content creation tools are equipped with SEO optimization features. They can analyze keywords, suggest meta tags, and help you structure your content for better search engine visibility.
This SEO optimization contributes to the discoverability of your content, making it more accessible to your target audience.

8. Social Media Management

For social media enthusiasts and marketers, AI streamlines content creation and scheduling. AI tools can generate social media posts, recommend optimal posting times, and analyze engagement metrics.
This automation ensures that your social media presence remains active and engaging, even during busy days.

9. Accessibility and Inclusivity
AI-powered content creation also promotes accessibility and inclusivity. Text-to-speech and speech-to-text technologies make content accessible to individuals with visual or hearing impairments.
By ensuring that content is available in various formats, AI enhances inclusivity and ensures that everyone can access and engage with the information.

10. Data-Driven Insights
AI analyzes user engagement and content performance data to provide insights and recommendations. Content creators can use these insights to refine their strategies and produce content that resonates with their audience. By harnessing data-driven insights, you can continuously improve your content quality and effectiveness.

While AI-enhanced content creation offers numerous advantages, it's important to maintain a balance between automation and human creativity. AI can assist in content generation, but it's essential to infuse your unique voice, style, and creativity into your work.

In conclusion, AI-powered content creation is a transformative force that significantly improves our daily lives by enhancing creativity, productivity, and accessibility. Whether you're a content creator, marketer, student, or simply someone who enjoys sharing ideas, AI ensures that you have the tools to produce high-quality content efficiently. As AI technology continues to advance, the future of content creation holds the promise of even more intelligent and context-aware tools, further empowering individuals and businesses to express themselves and engage with their audience in innovative ways.

Scanning the Future: How AI-Powered Document Scanning Transforms Your Daily Life

Document scanning is an essential task in both personal and professional settings, and it plays a significant role in our daily lives. However, the integration of Artificial Intelligence (AI) into document scanning has revolutionized the way we digitize, manage, and access information. AI-powered document scanning offers numerous benefits that enhance our daily routines, streamline workflows, and boost productivity. Here's how:

1. Enhanced OCR (Optical Character Recognition)
One of the most noticeable ways AI improves your daily life is by enhancing Optical Character Recognition (OCR) capabilities. AI-driven OCR technology can accurately recognize and convert printed or handwritten text into machine-readable text.
Imagine effortlessly converting handwritten notes into editable digital documents or quickly extracting text from printed books for research purposes. AI ensures that you can digitize and work with text-based information more efficiently.

2. Efficient Document Organization
AI-powered document scanning apps and software offer efficient document organization features. These tools can automatically categorize and tag documents based on content, date, keywords, or user-defined criteria.
Whether you're managing personal files, organizing business documents, or keeping track of receipts and bills, AI streamlines the process by helping you find and access the documents you need with ease.

3. Intelligent Search

Searching for specific information within a large collection of documents can be time-consuming. AI-driven document scanning tools enable intelligent search capabilities. They can identify keywords, phrases, and even context within scanned documents.

This feature allows you to quickly locate specific information, reducing the frustration of sifting through stacks of paper or digital files.

4. Improved Data Extraction

In professional settings, data extraction from documents is a common task, especially in industries like finance, healthcare, and legal services. AI-enhanced document scanning tools can automatically extract structured data, such as names, dates, addresses, and numerical values. This capability simplifies data entry tasks, minimizes errors, and accelerates data processing, making daily workflows more efficient.

5. Enhanced Security

AI-powered document scanning often includes advanced security features. These tools can encrypt scanned documents, apply access controls, and detect sensitive information to ensure compliance with data privacy regulations.

This enhanced security protects your personal and confidential information, giving you peace of mind in your daily document management.

6. Mobile Scanning Apps
AI-powered mobile scanning apps have become indispensable for individuals on the go. These apps turn your smartphone into a portable scanner, allowing you to capture documents, receipts, or whiteboard notes anytime, anywhere.
This convenience ensures that you can digitize important information on the spot, reducing clutter and preventing the loss of valuable documents.

7. Language Translation
For individuals dealing with multilingual documents, AI-powered document scanning can provide real-time language translation. These tools can translate scanned text into your preferred language, breaking down language barriers.
Whether you're traveling, conducting business internationally, or studying foreign-language documents, AI ensures that language is no longer a barrier to understanding and accessing information.

8. Accessibility for Individuals with Disabilities
AI-driven document scanning tools promote accessibility for individuals with disabilities. They can convert scanned text into audio formats, making documents accessible to those with visual impairments.

This inclusivity feature ensures that everyone has equal access to information, enhancing daily life for individuals with disabilities.

9. Cloud Integration
AI-enhanced document scanning often integrates seamlessly with cloud storage solutions. This means that scanned documents can be automatically uploaded and stored in the cloud, ensuring that your information is securely backed up and accessible from any device with an internet connection.
This cloud integration enhances collaboration and ensures that your documents are never lost or inaccessible.

10. Enhanced Collaboration
In professional settings, AI-powered document scanning enhances collaboration by enabling easy sharing and collaboration on digital documents. Documents can be scanned, edited, annotated, and shared with colleagues or clients in real time.
This collaboration feature streamlines work processes, reduces paperwork, and promotes efficient teamwork.

While AI-enhanced document scanning offers numerous benefits, it's essential to ensure the security of sensitive information and to use these tools responsibly. It's also important to periodically review and clean up digitized documents to avoid digital clutter.

In conclusion, AI-powered document scanning is a transformative force that significantly improves our daily lives by simplifying document management, boosting productivity, and promoting accessibility and inclusivity. Whether you're a student, a professional, or an individual seeking to organize personal documents, AI ensures that you can handle documents efficiently and access information with ease. As AI technology continues to advance, the future of document scanning holds the promise of even more intelligent and context-aware tools, further enhancing our daily routines and work processes.

Tracking Your Way to Financial Freedom: How AI-Enhanced Expense Tracking Improves Your Daily Life

Managing expenses is an integral part of our daily lives. Whether you're budgeting for personal expenses, running a household, or managing finances for a business, tracking expenses can be a daunting task. Fortunately, the integration of Artificial Intelligence (AI) into expense tracking has transformed the way we monitor, analyze, and manage our financial resources. AI-powered expense tracking offers numerous advantages that enhance our daily routines, promote financial well-being, and simplify financial decision-making. Here's how:

1. Automated Expense Tracking
One of the most noticeable ways AI improves your daily life is through automated expense tracking. AI-powered apps and software can automatically categorize and record expenses based on transaction data. This means no more manual data entry or tedious paperwork. Imagine all your expenses, from groceries to utility bills and even small daily purchases, being effortlessly recorded and organized for you. AI ensures that you can maintain a comprehensive and up-to-date record of your financial transactions without the hassle.

2. Real-Time Expense Monitoring
AI-driven expense tracking provides real-time monitoring of your financial transactions. These tools can send instant notifications when you make a purchase or receive money, helping you stay on top of your finances.
This feature ensures that you're always aware of your financial situation, allowing you to make informed spending decisions throughout the day.

3. Budgeting Assistance

Creating and sticking to a budget can be challenging. AI-powered expense tracking apps can help you set and maintain budgets by analyzing your spending patterns and suggesting budget adjustments.

Imagine receiving personalized budget recommendations based on your income and spending habits. AI ensures that you can budget effectively and work towards your financial goals.

4. Expense Categorization

AI-enhanced expense tracking categorizes expenses with a high degree of accuracy. These tools can recognize patterns and assign expenses to specific categories such as groceries, transportation, entertainment, and more.

This categorization simplifies the process of understanding where your money is going, allowing you to identify areas where you can potentially cut costs or allocate funds more effectively.

5. Savings Suggestions

AI-driven expense tracking can analyze your spending habits and offer suggestions on how to save money.

These suggestions may include alternatives to expensive purchases, discounts, or budget-friendly options.

This feature helps you make smarter spending choices, save money, and work towards your financial goals more efficiently.

6. Investment Insights

For those interested in investments, AI-enhanced expense tracking can provide insights into investment opportunities and strategies. These tools can analyze your financial situation and suggest investment options that align with your goals and risk tolerance.

This investment guidance ensures that you can make informed decisions when it comes to growing your wealth.

7. Tax Preparation

Expense tracking is a crucial part of tax preparation. AI-powered expense tracking tools can organize your financial records and generate reports that make tax filing easier.

Imagine having all your deductible expenses neatly categorized and calculated, ready for tax season. AI simplifies the process, helping you maximize your deductions and reduce tax-related stress.

8. Fraud Detection

AI can enhance security by detecting unusual or fraudulent transactions. AI-driven expense tracking apps can identify suspicious activity and send alerts when they detect potentially fraudulent transactions.

This security feature protects your financial accounts and ensures that your hard-earned money is safe from unauthorized access.

9. Credit Score Improvement
A good credit score is essential for various financial transactions, including loans and credit card applications. AI-enhanced expense tracking can offer insights into improving your credit score by suggesting strategies to reduce debt and manage credit responsibly.
This guidance helps you maintain a healthy credit profile, which is essential for financial stability.

10. Family and Business Expense Management
Expense tracking is not limited to personal finances. AI-powered tools can also assist in managing family or business expenses. These tools can provide a consolidated view of expenses, making it easier to track spending for multiple individuals or departments. Whether you're managing a household budget or tracking business expenses, AI ensures that you have the tools to maintain financial transparency and control.

While AI-enhanced expense tracking offers numerous benefits, it's important to use these tools responsibly and maintain awareness of your financial situation. AI can assist in managing expenses, but it's essential to make informed financial decisions based on your individual circumstances and goals.

In conclusion, AI-powered expense tracking is a transformative force that significantly improves our daily lives by simplifying financial management, promoting financial well-being, and streamlining financial decision-making. Whether you're a budget-conscious individual, a business owner, or someone seeking to take control of their finances, AI ensures that you can monitor and manage your expenses efficiently. As AI technology continues to advance, the future of expense tracking holds the promise of even more intelligent and context-aware tools, further enhancing our daily routines and financial stability.

Unlocking a World of Opportunities: How AI-Enhanced Language Learning Transforms Your Daily Life

Language learning is a journey that opens doors to new cultures, opportunities, and connections. Whether you're learning a new language for travel, career advancement, or personal enrichment, Artificial Intelligence (AI) is revolutionizing the way we acquire and master languages. AI-powered language learning tools are significantly improving our daily lives by making language learning more accessible, personalized, and effective. Here's how:

1. Personalized Learning Paths
One of the most noticeable ways AI improves your daily life is by tailoring language learning to your specific needs and goals. AI-powered language learning platforms use algorithms to assess your current proficiency level and learning preferences.
Imagine having a personalized curriculum that adapts to your pace, interests, and strengths. AI ensures that you receive a customized learning experience, maximizing your progress and motivation.

2. Real-Time Feedback
AI-driven language learning apps provide real-time feedback on pronunciation, grammar, and vocabulary usage. These tools use speech recognition and natural language processing to evaluate your spoken and written language.
This instant feedback allows you to correct mistakes and refine your language skills as you go, enhancing your daily language learning practice.

3. Immersive Language Experiences
Learning a language becomes more engaging with AI-powered immersive experiences. Language learning apps

can create virtual environments where you can practice conversational skills with AI-driven characters.
Imagine having interactive conversations in your target language, simulating real-life scenarios like ordering food in a restaurant or navigating a foreign city. AI ensures that you gain practical language skills through immersive experiences.

4. Enhanced Vocabulary Building
AI-enhanced language learning platforms offer advanced vocabulary building features. These tools curate word lists and flashcards based on your interests and learning objectives.
This feature helps you expand your vocabulary efficiently and focus on words that are relevant to your daily life and goals.

5. Language Exchange Partners
Connecting with native speakers for language practice is a valuable part of language learning. AI-powered platforms can match you with language exchange partners who share your interests and language goals.
This facilitates meaningful language exchanges, allowing you to practice speaking and improve cultural understanding with native speakers.

6. Adaptive Assessments

Regular assessments are crucial to track your language proficiency. AI-driven assessments can adapt to your skill level, providing accurate evaluations of your progress.
Imagine taking quizzes and tests that adjust in difficulty based on your performance, ensuring that you're continually challenged and making measurable progress in your daily language learning.

7. Multi-Language Support

AI-powered language learning tools often support multiple languages, making it easier for individuals interested in learning more than one language simultaneously.
This multi-language support caters to diverse interests and provides a well-rounded language learning experience.

8. Accessibility for Diverse Learning Styles

AI-enhanced language learning accommodates various learning styles. Visual learners can benefit from interactive exercises and videos, while auditory learners can focus on pronunciation and listening exercises.
AI ensures that you can choose the learning methods that suit your preferences and strengths.

9. Gamification and Motivation

Learning a language can be challenging, but AI-powered language learning apps make it fun through gamification. These apps use game elements like rewards, points, and challenges to motivate and engage learners.

This gamified approach transforms language learning into an enjoyable daily activity that keeps you motivated and eager to progress.

10. Continuous Learning Support
AI doesn't stop once you've achieved a certain proficiency level. These tools provide continuous learning support with advanced lessons, cultural insights, and access to authentic content like books, news articles, and podcasts in your target language.

This ensures that language learning remains a lifelong journey, enriching your daily life with new linguistic skills and cultural insights.

While AI-enhanced language learning offers numerous advantages, it's essential to combine technology with real-world language practice. Engaging in conversations, watching movies, and reading books in your target language are essential components of language acquisition.

In conclusion, AI-powered language learning is a transformative force that significantly improves our daily lives by making language acquisition accessible, personalized, and engaging. Whether you're learning a language for travel, business, or personal enrichment, AI ensures that you have the tools and support to achieve your language goals effectively. As AI technology continues to advance, the future of language learning holds the promise of even more intelligent and immersive experiences, fostering greater cultural understanding and global communication.

A Lens to the Future: How AI-Powered Cameras Revolutionize Your Daily Life

In an age where every moment is captured and shared, cameras have become an integral part of our daily lives. From preserving cherished memories to enhancing security, cameras play diverse roles. The integration of Artificial Intelligence (AI) into cameras has elevated their capabilities, offering a wide array of benefits that improve our daily routines, safety, and overall experience. Here's how AI-powered cameras are transforming our lives:

1. Enhanced Photography
One of the most noticeable ways AI improves your daily life is by enhancing photography. AI-powered cameras

can automatically adjust settings such as exposure, focus, and white balance to capture perfect shots in varying conditions.

Imagine taking professional-quality photos without the need for manual adjustments, even in challenging lighting or weather conditions. AI ensures that your everyday photography becomes effortless and stunning.

2. Intelligent Object Recognition

AI-powered cameras excel in object recognition. These cameras can identify and tag objects, people, and animals within a frame. This feature simplifies photo organization and makes it easier to search for specific images in your photo library.

With AI, you can quickly find all the photos of your beloved pet, your favorite landmarks, or even specific friends and family members.

3. Real-Time Image Enhancement

AI-driven cameras offer real-time image enhancement. Whether you're capturing a selfie or a scenic view, these cameras can improve image quality by reducing noise, enhancing colors, and sharpening details on the fly. This feature ensures that your photos and videos consistently look their best, making your visual memories even more vibrant and appealing.

4. Automatic Framing and Composition

Composition is key to great photography, but not everyone has the skills to frame a perfect shot. AI-powered cameras can analyze scenes and suggest optimal framing and composition for your photos. Imagine never having to worry about centering a subject or adjusting angles. AI ensures that your photos are beautifully composed, even if you're not a professional photographer.

5. Smart Facial Recognition

AI-enhanced cameras often feature facial recognition technology. They can identify and tag individuals in your photos, making it easy to organize and locate pictures of specific people.

This simplifies the process of creating photo albums or sharing pictures with friends and family, enhancing your daily photo management.

6. Security and Surveillance

AI-powered cameras have revolutionized security and surveillance systems. These cameras can detect and alert you to unusual or suspicious activities, whether it's at your home, office, or in public spaces.

Imagine receiving a notification when someone approaches your front door or when a security breach is detected in a restricted area. AI ensures that you can monitor your surroundings with greater peace of mind.

7. Smart Home Integration

AI-powered cameras can integrate seamlessly into smart home ecosystems. They can work with voice assistants and other smart devices to enhance your daily life.
For example, you can use voice commands to view live camera feeds on your smart TV, or receive notifications on your smartphone when a camera detects movement at your front door.

8. Wildlife and Nature Observation

For nature enthusiasts and wildlife photographers, AI-powered cameras are invaluable. These cameras can automatically detect and capture images of birds, animals, and natural phenomena like meteor showers or eclipses.
This feature transforms your daily nature excursions into opportunities to capture breathtaking moments with ease.

9. Language Translation

AI-powered cameras can also assist with language translation. They can scan and translate text from one language to another in real time, whether it's a street sign, menu, or document.
This capability makes traveling and exploring new places more accessible and enjoyable, as you can quickly understand and communicate with locals.

10. Health and Well-Being Monitoring

AI-powered cameras have applications in health and well-being. They can track vital signs, detect changes in skin tone, or monitor physical activity.

Imagine having a camera that can assess your overall well-being and suggest adjustments to your daily routine for a healthier lifestyle. AI ensures that you can prioritize your health seamlessly.

In conclusion, AI-powered cameras are a transformative force that significantly improves our daily lives by enhancing photography, security, convenience, and accessibility. Whether you're capturing memories, ensuring safety, or exploring the world, AI ensures that your camera experience is enriched with intelligence and functionality. As AI technology continues to advance, the future of AI-powered cameras holds the promise of even more intelligent and context-aware features, further enhancing our visual and security experiences.

The Brush of Tomorrow: How AI-Generated Art Transforms Your Daily Life

Art has always held a special place in human culture, enriching our lives with creativity and expression. With the advent of Artificial Intelligence (AI), the world of art is undergoing a remarkable transformation. AI-generated art is revolutionizing the way we create, appreciate, and interact with artistic works, and it has profound implications for our daily lives. Here's how AI-generated art is making its mark:

1. Democratizing Artistic Expression

One of the most significant ways AI improves your daily life is by democratizing artistic expression. AI-powered art tools enable anyone, regardless of their artistic skill or background, to become a creator.

Imagine turning your ideas into stunning artworks with the help of AI, whether it's a digital painting, a piece of music, or even a design for your living space. AI ensures that artistic expression becomes accessible to all.

2. Inspiring Creativity

AI-generated art inspires creativity by offering new perspectives and possibilities. AI algorithms can generate novel artistic concepts, pushing the boundaries of traditional art forms.

This inspiration can ignite your own creativity, encouraging you to explore new artistic horizons and infuse fresh ideas into your daily life.

3. Customized Artworks

AI-powered art tools can create customized artworks tailored to your preferences. These tools can generate art pieces that match your color schemes, themes, or personal tastes.

Imagine having a unique piece of art that complements your home decor or represents your individual style. AI ensures that art becomes a personal and meaningful part of your daily environment.

4. Art for Wellness

Art has a profound impact on mental well-being. AI-generated art can curate calming and visually pleasing artworks that promote relaxation and stress relief.

Imagine having a piece of AI-generated art on your wall that changes to match your mood or to create a serene atmosphere in your living space. AI ensures that art becomes a source of emotional well-being in your daily life.

5. Preservation and Restoration

AI is also playing a pivotal role in art preservation and restoration. AI algorithms can analyze deteriorated artworks and suggest restoration techniques.

This ensures that the world's cultural heritage is preserved for future generations and that you can continue to enjoy and learn from timeless masterpieces.

6. Art Recommender Systems

AI-powered art recommender systems analyze your art preferences and recommend artworks, artists, or styles that align with your taste.
Imagine discovering new artists or art movements that resonate with you, enriching your art appreciation and collection. AI ensures that you can explore the vast world of art effortlessly.

7. Personalized Gifts
AI-generated art can be a source of personalized gifts. AI-powered tools can create unique artworks for special occasions like birthdays, anniversaries, or weddings. Imagine gifting a loved one a piece of art generated by AI that celebrates your shared memories or reflects their personality. AI ensures that your gifts become thoughtful and meaningful expressions of love and appreciation.

8. Art in Augmented Reality
Augmented Reality (AR) powered by AI allows you to interact with art in new and immersive ways. AR apps can overlay AI-generated art onto your surroundings, turning your home into an ever-changing art gallery. This integration of art into your physical environment enhances your daily life by creating dynamic and visually captivating spaces.

9. Art and Education

AI-generated art can play a role in education. Teachers and students can use AI-generated art as a tool for learning and creative exploration.
Imagine using AI-generated art to teach art history, inspire artistic projects, or illustrate complex concepts in various subjects. AI ensures that art becomes an educational resource that enriches your daily learning experiences.

10. Cultural Exchange
AI-generated art transcends cultural boundaries. These artworks can incorporate elements from different cultures and traditions, fostering cross-cultural understanding and appreciation.
Imagine experiencing art that seamlessly blends diverse influences, promoting cultural exchange and unity. AI ensures that art becomes a bridge between cultures in your daily life.

In conclusion, AI-generated art is a transformative force that significantly improves our daily lives by democratizing creativity, inspiring innovation, and enhancing our environment with personalized and meaningful artworks. Whether you're an art enthusiast, a creative individual, or someone seeking to infuse your daily life with beauty and inspiration, AI ensures that art becomes an integral and accessible part of your world.

As AI technology continues to advance, the future of AI-generated art holds the promise of even more intricate, imaginative, and personalized creations, further enriching our daily lives with artistic wonders.

Leveling Up Leisure: How AI in Gaming Elevates Your Daily Life

Gaming has evolved from a simple pastime into a multi-billion-dollar industry that transcends age, gender, and geography. With the integration of Artificial Intelligence (AI), gaming experiences have been elevated to unprecedented heights, making a profound impact on our daily lives. Whether you're a casual gamer or a dedicated enthusiast, AI in gaming is transforming the way we play, interact, and immerse ourselves in virtual worlds. Here's how:

1. Immersive Gameplay
One of the most noticeable ways AI improves your daily life is by creating more immersive gameplay experiences. AI algorithms power realistic graphics, dynamic environments, and lifelike characters that respond to your actions.
Imagine exploring a virtual world where every detail is meticulously crafted, from the rustling leaves in the

forest to the expressions on the faces of in-game characters. AI ensures that gaming becomes an extraordinary adventure that transports you to another realm.

2. Adaptive Gameplay

AI-driven game systems adapt to your skill level and preferences, offering tailored challenges and experiences. Whether you're a novice or a seasoned player, AI ensures that you're always engaged and appropriately challenged.

Imagine playing a game that adjusts its difficulty in real-time based on your performance, ensuring that you remain engrossed without feeling overwhelmed or bored. AI ensures that gaming remains enjoyable and accessible for players of all levels.

3. Intelligent NPCs (Non-Playable Characters)

AI enhances the intelligence of NPCs in games, making them more responsive and lifelike. NPCs can exhibit complex behaviors, engage in realistic conversations, and adapt to your choices within the game.

Imagine interacting with NPCs that remember your previous encounters and have their own motivations and personalities. AI ensures that the gaming world feels vibrant and interactive, as if you're part of a living story.

4. Personalized Storytelling

AI in gaming enables personalized storytelling. These systems analyze your gameplay choices and adapt the game's narrative accordingly, creating unique and tailored experiences.

Imagine playing a game where your decisions shape the outcome, leading to multiple story branches and endings. AI ensures that gaming narratives are dynamic and reflective of your choices, enhancing replayability and immersion.

5. Realistic Physics and Simulation

AI-powered physics engines in games create realistic and dynamic environments. From the way objects interact with each other to the behavior of fluids and gases, AI-driven physics engines provide an authentic experience.

Imagine playing a racing game where vehicles handle realistically, or a first-person shooter where the impact of bullets on surfaces is accurate and visually stunning. AI ensures that gaming environments feel tangible and dynamic.

6. Natural Language Processing

AI-driven games often feature natural language processing (NLP) for voice commands and in-game interactions. This technology allows you to communicate with in-game characters, issue commands, and even engage in conversations.

Imagine conversing with characters in a game using your voice, directing your virtual team in real-time, or solving puzzles through spoken commands. AI ensures that gaming becomes more interactive and responsive to your voice.

7. Streamlined Multiplayer Experiences
AI can enhance multiplayer gaming by optimizing matchmaking, balancing teams, and detecting cheating or abusive behavior. These AI systems create fair and enjoyable multiplayer environments.
Imagine playing an online game where matches are skillfully balanced, ensuring competitive and enjoyable gameplay. AI ensures that multiplayer gaming remains engaging and free from unfair advantages.

8. Advanced Graphics Rendering
AI-driven graphics rendering techniques generate stunning visuals. AI can upscale lower-resolution textures, eliminate graphical artifacts, and deliver high-quality graphics even on less powerful hardware.
Imagine playing games with breathtaking graphics that push the boundaries of realism and detail. AI ensures that gaming visuals are visually striking, regardless of your gaming platform.

9. Predictive Analytics

AI can analyze your gaming behavior to offer personalized recommendations and suggestions. These systems can recommend new games, in-game items, or strategies based on your preferences and playstyle. Imagine receiving game recommendations that align perfectly with your gaming interests, ensuring that you never run out of exciting titles to explore. AI ensures that gaming remains a continuously enriching experience.

10. Game Testing and Development
AI is also used in game development to streamline testing processes. AI-driven testing tools can identify bugs, glitches, and balance issues, ensuring that games are more stable and enjoyable upon release.

Imagine playing games that undergo rigorous testing, resulting in smoother gameplay and fewer technical issues. AI ensures that game developers can deliver high-quality experiences to players.

In conclusion, AI in gaming is a transformative force that significantly improves our daily lives by creating more immersive, personalized, and engaging gaming experiences. Whether you're a casual gamer or a dedicated enthusiast, AI ensures that gaming becomes an extraordinary adventure that transports you to another realm. As AI technology continues to advance, the future of gaming holds the promise of even more intelligent, lifelike, and interactive experiences, further enriching our daily lives in the virtual world.

Beyond Reality: How AI-Enhanced Virtual Reality Transforms Your Daily Life

Virtual Reality (VR) has emerged as a game-changer in the world of technology, offering immersive experiences that transport us to entirely new realms. The integration of Artificial Intelligence (AI) with VR is taking this innovation to new heights, profoundly impacting our daily lives. From entertainment to education, healthcare to workplace collaboration, AI-powered VR is redefining how we interact with the digital world. Here's how:

1. Immersive Entertainment
One of the most noticeable ways AI improves your daily life is through immersive entertainment experiences in VR. AI algorithms enhance VR content by generating realistic graphics, lifelike characters, and dynamic environments.
Imagine stepping into a virtual world where you can explore alien planets, battle dragons, or attend a live concert, all with an unparalleled level of immersion. AI

ensures that your entertainment becomes an extraordinary adventure that transcends reality.

2. Personalized Learning and Training
AI-powered VR is revolutionizing education and training. It offers personalized learning experiences, adapting content and difficulty levels to individual learners. This technology has applications in classrooms, job training, and skill development.
Imagine students learning complex concepts by interacting with 3D models or employees practicing emergency procedures in a virtual environment. AI ensures that learning and training become more engaging and effective.

3. Healthcare and Therapy
VR combined with AI has transformative potential in healthcare. Virtual reality therapy is being used to treat various conditions, including post-traumatic stress disorder (PTSD), phobias, and chronic pain.
Imagine patients receiving therapy by immersing themselves in VR environments that help them confront and overcome their fears or manage pain. AI ensures that healthcare becomes more accessible and effective, especially for mental health and rehabilitation.

4. Architectural Design and Visualization

AI-enhanced VR is changing the way architects and designers work. It allows professionals to create and explore detailed 3D models of buildings and spaces in a virtual environment, making the design process more efficient and collaborative.

Imagine architects and clients walking through a virtual representation of a building, making real-time design decisions and adjustments. AI ensures that architectural design and visualization become more interactive and visually engaging.

5. Enhanced Remote Collaboration

AI-powered VR enables remote collaboration that feels as if you're in the same room. Virtual meetings in VR can provide a sense of presence and spatial awareness, making collaboration more effective.

Imagine attending virtual meetings where you can see and interact with colleagues as if they were physically present, improving communication and fostering teamwork. AI ensures that remote collaboration becomes more engaging and productive.

6. Gaming Beyond Limits

AI-driven VR gaming offers realistic and dynamic experiences that adapt to your gameplay. NPCs in VR games can exhibit complex behaviors, enhancing immersion and making gaming more challenging.

Imagine playing a VR game where AI-controlled characters respond intelligently to your actions and adapt their strategies in real-time. AI ensures that gaming in VR becomes an extraordinary adventure that tests your skills and wits.

7. Cultural and Historical Exploration
AI-enhanced VR can take you on virtual journeys through historical sites and cultural landmarks. It can recreate ancient cities, museums, and historical events, providing educational and enriching experiences. Imagine walking through the streets of ancient Rome or exploring the Pyramids of Giza from the comfort of your home. AI ensures that cultural and historical exploration becomes an immersive and informative endeavor.

8. Enhanced Communication
AI-powered VR can enhance communication by providing expressive avatars and real-time language translation. This technology bridges language barriers and fosters more engaging virtual interactions. Imagine conversing with people from around the world in VR, with AI translating your speech into different languages and rendering lifelike avatars that convey your emotions. AI ensures that communication becomes more inclusive and accessible.

9. Environmental Simulation

AI-driven VR can simulate various environments, from the depths of the ocean to outer space. This has applications in scientific research, environmental conservation, and astronaut training.
Imagine scientists exploring the ocean's depths or astronauts practicing spacewalks in VR simulations that closely mimic real conditions. AI ensures that environmental simulation becomes a valuable tool for research and training.

10. Accessibility and Inclusivity
AI-enhanced VR can make digital experiences more accessible to individuals with disabilities. It can provide assistive features such as voice commands, haptic feedback, and gesture recognition.

Imagine individuals with mobility impairments enjoying VR experiences through voice commands or individuals with visual impairments exploring VR environments with audio descriptions. AI ensures that VR becomes more inclusive and enriching for everyone.

In conclusion, AI-powered VR is a transformative force that significantly improves our daily lives by offering immersive entertainment, personalized learning, healthcare solutions, and enhanced collaboration. Whether you're seeking entertainment, education, or professional development, AI ensures that VR becomes an extraordinary tool for experiencing and interacting with the digital world. As AI technology continues to advance, the future of AI-enhanced VR holds the promise of even more realistic, interactive, and innovative experiences, further enriching our daily lives in the virtual realm.

Your Partner in Career Advancement: How AI Enhances Job Searching

The job market is dynamic and competitive, and job searching can often feel like a daunting task. However, the integration of Artificial Intelligence (AI) into the job-searching process is revolutionizing the way individuals find new opportunities, plan their careers, and make informed decisions. AI-driven job searching tools offer a wide range of benefits that significantly improve your daily life, whether you're actively seeking a new position or just curious about the job market. Here's how:

1. Personalized Job Recommendations
One of the most noticeable ways AI improves your daily life is through personalized job recommendations. AI algorithms analyze your skills, experience, and preferences to suggest job openings that match your profile.

Imagine receiving job recommendations tailored to your unique qualifications and career goals. AI ensures that you discover opportunities that are the best fit for you, making your job search more efficient and effective.

2. Resume Optimization

AI-driven tools can help you optimize your resume to increase your chances of getting noticed by employers. These tools analyze job descriptions and offer suggestions on how to tailor your resume to specific positions.

Imagine having your resume automatically adjusted to highlight the skills and experiences most relevant to the job you're applying for. AI ensures that your application stands out to potential employers.

3. Interview Preparation

Preparing for interviews can be nerve-wracking, but AI-powered interview preparation tools can help. They provide sample interview questions, offer tips on answering common interview queries, and even simulate interview scenarios to practice.

Imagine having access to a virtual interview coach that helps you refine your interview skills and boost your confidence. AI ensures that you are well-prepared for job interviews, increasing your chances of success.

4. Skills Gap Analysis

AI can analyze your current skill set and identify areas where you may have skill gaps. This information can help you make informed decisions about further education or training to enhance your qualifications. Imagine receiving insights into the skills that are in high demand in your field and personalized recommendations for upskilling. AI ensures that you can continuously improve your skills and stay competitive in the job market.

5. Networking Opportunities

AI-driven platforms can connect you with relevant professionals and industry peers, helping you expand your professional network. These platforms can suggest networking events, webinars, or conferences based on your interests and career goals.

Imagine having access to a network of professionals who can provide advice, mentorship, or even job referrals. AI ensures that you can build meaningful connections and leverage them for career growth.

6. Salary Insights

AI-powered job searching tools often provide salary insights for specific roles and industries. You can get an idea of salary ranges for different positions, helping you negotiate better compensation packages.

Imagine having data at your fingertips that allows you to negotiate your salary with confidence, ensuring that you're fairly compensated for your skills and experience. AI ensures that you can make informed decisions about your earning potential.

7. Job Market Trends

AI can analyze job market trends and provide insights into which industries are growing, which skills are in demand, and where job opportunities are concentrated. This information can help you make informed decisions about your career path.

Imagine having access to real-time data that guides your career choices, ensuring that you align your skills and aspirations with market demands. AI ensures that you can plan your career strategically.

8. Job Application Tracking

AI-driven job searching platforms often offer features to track your job applications. You can keep tabs on the positions you've applied for, receive status updates, and set reminders for follow-ups.

Imagine having a centralized dashboard that streamlines your job application process, reducing the risk of missing out on opportunities. AI ensures that you can manage your job search efficiently.

9. Company Culture Insights

AI can provide insights into company cultures based on employee reviews and feedback. This information can help you assess whether a potential employer's values and work environment align with your preferences. Imagine having access to employee reviews and ratings that give you a glimpse into what it's like to work at a particular company. AI ensures that you can make informed decisions about the workplace culture you want to be a part of.

10. Diversity and Inclusion
AI-driven job searching platforms are increasingly focused on promoting diversity and inclusion. They may provide information about a company's diversity initiatives, policies, and inclusivity ratings.

Imagine having access to data that helps you identify organizations committed to diversity and inclusion, allowing you to choose employers that align with your values. AI ensures that you can support and contribute to diverse workplaces.

In conclusion, AI-powered job searching is a transformative force that significantly improves your daily life by personalizing job recommendations, optimizing your resume, preparing you for interviews, and providing valuable insights into the job market. Whether you're actively job hunting or planning your career path, AI ensures that you have the tools and information to make informed decisions and achieve your professional goals. As AI technology continues to advance, the future of job searching holds the promise of even more intelligent, personalized, and efficient tools, further enhancing your daily life in the world of work.

Navigating Your Financial Journey: How AI Enhances Daily Financial Planning

Managing personal finances can often be a complex and daunting task, but with the integration of Artificial Intelligence (AI), the world of financial planning has been revolutionized. AI-powered financial tools and services are significantly improving our daily lives by offering personalized insights, optimizing investments, and enhancing financial decision-making. Whether you're saving for retirement, managing debt, or planning for a major purchase, AI is a powerful ally on your financial journey. Here's how:

1. Personalized Budgeting
One of the most noticeable ways AI improves your daily life is through personalized budgeting assistance. AI algorithms analyze your income, expenses, and spending habits to create customized budgets that align with your financial goals.

Imagine having a budget that considers your unique circumstances and offers real-time suggestions to help you stay on track. AI ensures that your financial planning becomes more effective and tailored to your needs.

2. Expense Tracking and Categorization

AI-powered financial apps can automatically track and categorize your expenses. They use machine learning to recognize patterns in your spending, making it easier to see where your money is going.

Imagine effortlessly tracking your expenses without manual data entry, and receiving insights into your spending habits that can help you identify areas where you can save. AI ensures that you have a clearer picture of your financial health.

3. Investment Optimization

AI-driven investment platforms use algorithms to optimize your investment portfolio. They analyze market trends, your risk tolerance, and financial goals to suggest diversified investment strategies.

Imagine having an investment advisor that continually adjusts your portfolio to maximize returns while managing risk. AI ensures that your investments work smarter and harder for you.

4. Financial Goal Planning

AI-enhanced financial planning tools help you set and achieve financial goals. They provide insights into how much you need to save, offer investment strategies, and track your progress toward milestones.

Imagine having a roadmap to guide your financial journey, from saving for a down payment on a house to planning for a comfortable retirement. AI ensures that your financial goals become more achievable and well-defined.

5. Debt Management

AI-powered financial apps can assist with managing and paying down debt. They analyze your outstanding loans, interest rates, and payment history to create optimized debt repayment plans.

Imagine having a debt reduction strategy that minimizes interest costs and accelerates your path to debt-free living. AI ensures that you can take control of your financial obligations.

6. Automated Savings

AI-driven savings apps can automatically transfer funds into savings or investment accounts based on your income and spending patterns. These "micro-savings" strategies help you build wealth over time.

Imagine effortlessly saving for emergencies, retirement, or future goals without having to manually move money around. AI ensures that your savings grow consistently and purposefully.

7. Credit Score Improvement

AI-powered credit score monitoring tools can provide insights into factors affecting your credit score and suggest actions to improve it. This can help you secure better loan terms and financial opportunities.

Imagine having a tool that guides you toward better credit health by identifying areas for improvement and tracking your progress. AI ensures that your financial well-being extends to your creditworthiness.

8. Fraud Detection and Security

AI plays a crucial role in financial security by identifying unusual or suspicious transactions and alerting you to potential fraud. These systems continuously monitor your accounts for unauthorized activity.

Imagine having a vigilant guardian that protects your financial assets and alerts you to potential threats in real-time. AI ensures that your financial transactions are secure and stress-free.

9. Tax Optimization

AI-driven tax preparation services can help you optimize your tax returns. They identify eligible deductions and credits, reducing your tax liability and ensuring you receive the maximum refund.

Imagine filing your taxes with confidence, knowing that you've taken advantage of all available tax-saving opportunities. AI ensures that you keep more of your hard-earned money.

10. Retirement Planning

AI-powered retirement planning tools can provide projections of your retirement savings and suggest adjustments to ensure a comfortable retirement. They consider factors like inflation and market fluctuations.

Imagine having a retirement planner that adjusts your savings strategy as your financial situation evolves, giving you peace of mind about your retirement goals. AI ensures that you're financially prepared for your golden years.

In conclusion, AI-enhanced financial planning is a transformative force that significantly improves your daily life by offering personalized budgeting, optimizing investments, and enhancing your financial well-being. Whether you're just starting to build your financial future or looking to optimize your existing financial strategies, AI ensures that you have the tools and insights to make informed decisions and secure your financial success. As AI technology continues to advance, the future of AI-driven financial planning holds the promise of even more intelligent, customized, and proactive financial guidance, further enhancing your daily life on your financial journey.

Illuminating Minds: How AI in Education Transforms Your Daily Learning Experience

Education is the cornerstone of personal and societal growth, and with the integration of Artificial Intelligence (AI), learning has taken on new dimensions. AI in education is significantly improving our daily lives by personalizing learning, enhancing teaching methods, and expanding access to quality education. Whether you're a student, teacher, or lifelong learner, AI is reshaping the way we acquire knowledge and skills. Here's how:

1. Personalized Learning Paths
One of the most noticeable ways AI improves your daily life is through personalized learning paths. AI algorithms analyze individual learning styles, strengths, and weaknesses to create customized curricula.
Imagine having an educational experience that caters to your unique needs and pace, ensuring that you grasp concepts thoroughly. AI ensures that learning becomes

tailored to your abilities, making it more effective and engaging.

2. Adaptive Assessments

AI-driven assessments adapt to each learner's level of proficiency. These assessments provide immediate feedback and adjust the difficulty of questions based on the learner's performance.

Imagine taking tests that challenge you at just the right level, helping you steadily progress and master subjects. AI ensures that assessments become a tool for growth rather than just evaluation.

3. Intelligent Tutoring

AI-powered tutoring systems offer real-time assistance to learners. They can answer questions, provide explanations, and offer guidance on coursework, enhancing the learning experience.

Imagine having a personal tutor available 24/7 to help you with homework, clarifications, and practice problems. AI ensures that learning becomes a continuous and well-supported journey.

4. Accessibility and Inclusivity

AI in education is making learning more accessible to individuals with disabilities. Text-to-speech and speech-to-text features, as well as other assistive technologies, enable a broader range of learners to participate.

Imagine students with visual impairments engaging in lessons through text-to-speech technology or individuals with dyslexia receiving tailored support. AI ensures that education becomes more inclusive and empowering.

5. Automating Administrative Tasks

AI can automate administrative tasks for teachers, such as grading assignments and tracking attendance. This frees up educators to focus more on teaching and individualized student support.

Imagine teachers spending less time on paperwork and more time engaging with students and enhancing their learning experiences. AI ensures that educators can maximize their impact.

6. Data-Driven Insights

AI analytics provide valuable data on student performance and engagement. Educators can use these insights to identify struggling students and implement targeted interventions.

Imagine teachers having access to real-time data that helps them understand each student's progress and adapt instruction accordingly. AI ensures that educators can provide timely support.

7. Language Learning and Translation

AI-driven language learning apps and translation tools make language acquisition more accessible. These tools can help learners develop language skills and facilitate communication in diverse languages.

Imagine using AI to learn a new language or communicate with people from different linguistic backgrounds effortlessly. AI ensures that language learning becomes more engaging and accessible.

8. Virtual Reality in Education

AI combined with Virtual Reality (VR) offers immersive educational experiences. Learners can explore historical sites, conduct virtual experiments, or interact with complex simulations.

Imagine students stepping into the shoes of historical figures or exploring distant planets through VR-enhanced lessons. AI ensures that education becomes more engaging and experiential.

9. Career Counseling and Guidance

AI can offer career counseling and guidance by analyzing a student's skills, interests, and market trends. This helps learners make informed decisions about their educational and career paths.

Imagine students receiving personalized recommendations for majors, courses, and career options that align with their passions and aptitudes. AI ensures that education becomes a pathway to fulfilling careers.

10. Lifelong Learning

AI-powered platforms facilitate lifelong learning by offering courses and resources that cater to individuals of all ages and backgrounds. Learning doesn't stop with formal education; it's a lifelong journey.

Imagine having access to a vast library of courses and resources that empower you to continually acquire new skills and knowledge. AI ensures that education becomes a lifelong pursuit of growth.

In conclusion, AI in education is a transformative force that significantly improves your daily life by personalizing learning, enhancing teaching methods, and expanding access to quality education. Whether you're a student, teacher, or lifelong learner, AI ensures that education becomes a dynamic and enriching journey. As AI technology continues to advance, the future of AI-driven education holds the promise of even more intelligent, adaptive, and accessible learning experiences, further enhancing your daily life as you continue to explore the world of knowledge and possibilities.

Elevating Customer Support: How AI Enhances Your Daily Experience

In the age of technology, customer support is undergoing a significant transformation, thanks to the integration of Artificial Intelligence (AI). AI-powered customer support solutions are revolutionizing the way businesses interact with their customers and, in turn, how you experience customer service in your daily life. Whether you're seeking assistance with a product, troubleshooting a technical issue, or simply seeking information, AI is reshaping the customer support landscape in remarkable ways. Here's how:

1. Instant Access to Information
One of the most noticeable ways AI improves your daily life is by providing instant access to information. AI-powered chatbots and virtual assistants can answer common queries, provide product details, and offer solutions to frequently encountered problems, 24/7. Imagine never having to wait on hold or navigate through a maze of menus when seeking assistance. AI ensures that you can access information swiftly and efficiently, making your interactions with businesses more seamless.

2. Efficient Issue Resolution
AI-driven customer support systems can resolve issues efficiently by diagnosing problems and offering step-by-step solutions. These systems can troubleshoot technical

glitches, guide you through fixes, or escalate complex issues to human agents when necessary.

Imagine having AI assist you in resolving issues with your smartphone, computer, or home appliances, making technical support more accessible and effective. AI ensures that your problems get solved promptly.

3. Personalized Assistance

AI analyzes customer data to provide personalized assistance. It can recognize your preferences, past interactions, and purchase history, allowing it to offer tailored recommendations or solutions.

Imagine receiving product recommendations or support based on your unique preferences and needs. AI ensures that your customer support experience becomes more individualized and relevant.

4. Reduced Wait Times

AI-driven chatbots and virtual assistants significantly reduce wait times when seeking assistance. You no longer have to endure long hold times on phone calls or wait for email responses.

Imagine getting immediate responses to your inquiries, whether it's about a product, a service, or a billing concern. AI ensures that your time is valued, making customer support more efficient.

5. Multilingual Support

AI can bridge language barriers by offering multilingual support. It can translate conversations in real-time, ensuring that businesses can assist customers from around the world.

Imagine being able to communicate with customer support representatives in your preferred language, no matter where you are or what language you speak. AI ensures that support becomes more accessible and inclusive.

6. Predictive Customer Service

AI analyzes customer behavior and usage patterns to predict potential issues before they occur. For example, it can detect irregularities in your utility usage and notify you of potential problems with your services.

Imagine receiving alerts about a potential internet outage or a malfunctioning appliance before it becomes a major inconvenience. AI ensures that customer service becomes proactive and anticipatory.

7. 24/7 Availability

AI-powered customer support operates 24/7, providing round-the-clock assistance. You can seek help or information at any time, whether it's during office hours or in the middle of the night.

Imagine being able to resolve issues or get answers to your questions at your convenience, without having to wait for business hours. AI ensures that customer support is available whenever you need it.

8. Data Security and Privacy

AI can enhance data security and privacy by verifying your identity through biometrics or multi-factor authentication. This ensures that your personal information remains protected during customer interactions.

Imagine feeling confident that your sensitive information is safeguarded when seeking support for financial matters or account-related issues. AI ensures that customer support is both convenient and secure.

9. Efficient Routing to Human Agents

AI can efficiently route inquiries to human agents when needed. It can recognize when a problem is too complex for automation and seamlessly transfer the conversation to a knowledgeable human representative.

Imagine having the best of both worlds—quick automated responses for straightforward questions and the expertise of a human agent for more complex issues. AI ensures that you receive the most appropriate assistance.

10. Continuous Improvement

AI continuously learns and adapts based on customer interactions, making customer support more effective over time. It can identify areas for improvement and refine its responses and recommendations.

Imagine a customer support system that gets better at assisting you with each interaction, ensuring a consistently high level of service. AI ensures that businesses can evolve and enhance their customer support offerings.

In conclusion, AI-powered customer support is a transformative force that significantly improves your daily life by providing instant access to information, efficient issue resolution, personalized assistance, reduced wait times, multilingual support, and much more. Whether you're seeking help from a retailer, a service provider, or a tech company, AI ensures that customer support becomes more efficient, accessible, and tailored to your needs. As AI technology continues to advance, the future of AI-driven customer support holds the promise of even smarter, more empathetic, and highly efficient interactions, further enhancing your daily experience with businesses and services.

Transforming Healthcare: How AI Enhances Your Daily Well-being

Healthcare is a fundamental aspect of our lives, and the integration of Artificial Intelligence (AI) is revolutionizing the healthcare industry, making it more efficient, accessible, and personalized. AI-driven healthcare solutions are significantly improving your daily life by enhancing medical diagnostics, optimizing treatment plans, and expanding access to quality healthcare services. Whether you're a patient, healthcare professional, or simply conscious of your well-being, AI is reshaping how we experience healthcare. Here's how:

1. Enhanced Medical Diagnostics
One of the most noticeable ways AI improves your daily life is by enhancing medical diagnostics. AI algorithms can analyze medical images, such as X-rays, MRIs, and CT scans, with remarkable accuracy, aiding in the early detection of diseases.
Imagine receiving more accurate and timely diagnoses, enabling early intervention and improving treatment outcomes. AI ensures that medical diagnostics become more reliable and efficient.

2. Personalized Treatment Plans
AI-powered healthcare systems can create personalized treatment plans based on your medical history, genetic makeup, and current health status. These plans consider individual factors to optimize treatment effectiveness and minimize side effects.

Imagine receiving treatment plans that are tailored specifically to your needs and genetic predispositions, improving your chances of a successful recovery. AI ensures that healthcare becomes more precise and patient-centric.

3. Predictive Healthcare Analytics
AI analyzes patient data to predict health trends and identify individuals at risk of specific diseases or health complications. Healthcare providers can use this information to offer preventive care and early interventions.
Imagine having a healthcare system that alerts you and your doctor to potential health risks, allowing for proactive measures to maintain your well-being. AI ensures that healthcare becomes more proactive and preventive.

4. Streamlined Administrative Tasks
AI can automate administrative tasks in healthcare, such as appointment scheduling, billing, and claims processing. This streamlines operations, reducing administrative burdens on healthcare professionals and ensuring smoother patient experiences.
Imagine spending less time on paperwork and more time interacting with healthcare providers during your visits. AI ensures that healthcare administration becomes more efficient and patient-focused.

5. Telemedicine and Remote Monitoring
AI facilitates telemedicine and remote monitoring, enabling you to receive medical consultations and monitoring from the comfort of your home. This is especially valuable for patients with chronic conditions. Imagine consulting with your healthcare provider through video calls or having your vital signs remotely monitored, reducing the need for frequent in-person visits. AI ensures that healthcare becomes more accessible and convenient.

6. Drug Discovery and Development
AI accelerates drug discovery and development by analyzing vast datasets and simulating drug interactions. This expedites the process of bringing new medications to market, potentially providing quicker access to life-saving treatments.
Imagine having access to innovative medications and therapies sooner, improving your chances of managing or recovering from illnesses. AI ensures that healthcare becomes more cutting-edge and responsive.

7. Patient Engagement and Education
AI-powered healthcare apps can engage patients by providing educational content, reminders for medications, and personalized health tips. This

encourages individuals to take an active role in managing their health.

Imagine receiving daily health insights and reminders that empower you to make informed choices about your well-being. AI ensures that healthcare becomes more engaging and educational.

8. Language Translation and Accessibility

AI-driven translation tools facilitate communication between healthcare providers and patients who speak different languages. This ensures that language barriers do not hinder access to healthcare services.

Imagine being able to communicate your medical concerns in your native language, regardless of where you seek healthcare services. AI ensures that healthcare becomes more inclusive and accessible to diverse populations.

9. Assistance for Healthcare Professionals

AI assists healthcare professionals in making informed decisions. It can provide relevant medical literature, suggest treatment options, and analyze patient data to support clinical decisions.

Imagine your doctor having access to AI tools that help them stay up-to-date with the latest research and provide the best possible care. AI ensures that healthcare professionals can enhance their expertise.

10. Healthcare Data Security and Privacy
AI can enhance data security and privacy in healthcare by monitoring for unauthorized access and identifying potential breaches. This safeguards sensitive patient information and ensures compliance with data protection regulations. Imagine feeling confident that your personal health data is protected, even as healthcare providers use AI to improve your care. AI ensures that healthcare remains both technologically advanced and secure.

In conclusion, AI in healthcare is a transformative force that significantly improves your daily life by enhancing medical diagnostics, optimizing treatment plans, and expanding access to quality healthcare services. Whether you're a patient seeking better care or a healthcare professional aiming to provide it, AI ensures that healthcare becomes more efficient, accessible, and patient-centered. As AI technology continues to advance, the future of AI-driven healthcare holds the promise of even more precise, personalized, and innovative approaches to maintaining and improving your well-being.

Cultivating the Future: How AI Revolutionizes Agriculture for Your Benefit

Agriculture is the bedrock of human civilization, and the integration of Artificial Intelligence (AI) is ushering in a new era of farming and food production. AI-powered agriculture is significantly improving your daily life by enhancing crop management, optimizing resource utilization, and ensuring food security. Whether you're a consumer, farmer, or environmentally conscious individual, AI is reshaping the way we experience agriculture. Here's how:

1. Precision Agriculture
One of the most noticeable ways AI improves your daily life is through precision agriculture. AI algorithms analyze data from satellites, drones, and sensors to monitor crop health, soil conditions, and weather patterns. Farmers can make data-driven decisions about planting, irrigation, and harvesting, optimizing resource use and increasing yields.
Imagine more efficient and sustainable farming practices that reduce the environmental impact of agriculture while ensuring a consistent food supply. AI ensures that agriculture becomes more precise and environmentally friendly.

2. Crop Monitoring and Disease Detection

AI-driven systems can continuously monitor crops for signs of disease, pests, or nutrient deficiencies. Early detection allows for timely intervention, reducing crop losses and the need for chemical treatments.

Imagine crops that are healthier, safer to eat, and cultivated with minimal chemical inputs. AI ensures that agriculture becomes more sustainable and produces safer food.

3. Predictive Analytics

AI analyzes historical and real-time data to provide farmers with predictive insights. This helps them anticipate changes in weather, market conditions, and crop yields, allowing for better planning and risk mitigation.

Imagine farmers making informed decisions that lead to more stable and profitable farming operations. AI ensures that agriculture becomes more resilient and less susceptible to unpredictable factors.

4. Autonomous Farming Equipment

AI-powered robots and drones can perform tasks like planting, harvesting, and weeding with precision and efficiency. These autonomous machines reduce the need for manual labor, making farming less labor-intensive and more productive.

Imagine a future where robots and drones handle the physical work on farms, freeing up farmers to focus on higher-level tasks and decision-making. AI ensures that agriculture becomes more efficient and less reliant on manual labor.

5. Water Management

AI helps optimize water usage in agriculture by monitoring soil moisture levels and controlling irrigation systems. This reduces water wastage and supports sustainable water management practices. Imagine a world where water resources are conserved, and agriculture doesn't strain local water supplies. AI ensures that agriculture becomes more water-efficient and environmentally responsible.

6. Livestock Health Monitoring

AI extends its benefits to animal agriculture by monitoring the health and well-being of livestock. Sensors and AI algorithms can detect signs of illness or distress in animals, allowing for prompt veterinary care. Imagine livestock that are healthier and raised under conditions that prioritize their well-being. AI ensures that animal agriculture becomes more humane and sustainable.

7. Food Supply Chain Optimization

AI optimizes the food supply chain, from production to distribution. It can predict demand, reduce food waste, and ensure that food reaches consumers more efficiently and safely.

Imagine a world with less food waste, where every step of the supply chain operates with precision to deliver fresh and safe products to your table. AI ensures that agriculture becomes more sustainable and less wasteful.

8. Environmental Conservation

AI can help farmers implement environmentally friendly practices by providing insights into sustainable farming techniques. This contributes to soil health, biodiversity conservation, and reduced carbon emissions. Imagine a world where agriculture coexists harmoniously with nature, contributing to the preservation of ecosystems. AI ensures that agriculture becomes more sustainable and ecologically responsible.

9. Global Food Security

AI plays a crucial role in ensuring global food security by increasing crop yields, optimizing resource use, and reducing losses due to pests and diseases. This helps address the challenges of feeding a growing population. Imagine a future where hunger and food shortages are mitigated by smart agricultural practices. AI ensures that agriculture becomes a cornerstone of global food security.

10. Agricultural Education and Training

AI-powered educational tools can help train the next generation of farmers and agricultural professionals. These tools provide access to knowledge and best practices, even in remote or underserved areas. Imagine a world where aspiring farmers have access to high-quality training and resources, enabling them to contribute to sustainable agriculture. AI ensures that agriculture becomes more inclusive and knowledge-driven.

In conclusion, AI-powered agriculture is a transformative force that significantly improves your daily life by enhancing crop management, optimizing resource utilization, and ensuring food security. Whether you're a consumer enjoying safer and more sustainable food or a farmer adopting innovative practices, AI ensures that agriculture becomes more efficient, environmentally responsible, and resilient in the face of global challenges. As AI technology continues to advance, the future of AI-driven agriculture holds the promise of even more precise, sustainable, and productive farming practices, further enhancing your daily life and the future of food production.

Navigating the Future: How AI Transforms Your Daily Commute and Travel

Transportation is an integral part of our daily lives, and the integration of Artificial Intelligence (AI) is revolutionizing how we move from place to place. AI-powered transportation systems are significantly enhancing your daily life by improving safety, efficiency, and convenience in various modes of transport. Whether you're a commuter, traveler, or just someone who values ease of movement, AI is reshaping the way we experience transportation. Here's how:

1. Safer Roads and Autonomous Vehicles
One of the most noticeable ways AI improves your daily life is through safer roads and autonomous vehicles. AI algorithms analyze real-time data from sensors, cameras, and radar to make split-second decisions that prevent accidents. Autonomous vehicles, equipped with AI, have the potential to reduce human errors and save lives on the road.
Imagine a daily commute where you can relax or work while your autonomous vehicle takes you to your destination safely. AI ensures that transportation becomes significantly safer and less stressful.

2. Traffic Management and Congestion Reduction

AI plays a pivotal role in optimizing traffic management systems. Smart traffic lights, powered by AI, can adapt to traffic flow in real-time, reducing congestion and minimizing wait times. AI also helps predict traffic patterns and suggests alternate routes to drivers.

Imagine a morning commute with minimal traffic jams, allowing you to reach your destination quickly and with less frustration. AI ensures that transportation becomes more efficient and less time-consuming.

3. Public Transportation Enhancements

AI improves the efficiency and reliability of public transportation systems. Smart schedules and predictive maintenance powered by AI ensure that buses and trains run on time. Additionally, AI can enhance the safety and security of public transportation through surveillance and real-time monitoring.

Imagine a daily commute where you can depend on public transportation for punctuality and safety, making your daily routine more predictable and enjoyable. AI ensures that public transportation becomes a more attractive option for commuters.

4. Ride-Sharing and Mobility as a Service (MaaS)

AI-powered ride-sharing services and Mobility as a Service platforms optimize the allocation of vehicles and routes. These services help reduce the number of cars on the road, ease traffic congestion, and lower carbon emissions.

Imagine a city with reduced traffic congestion and cleaner air due to increased carpooling and efficient transportation services. AI ensures that transportation becomes more environmentally friendly and sustainable.

5. Improved Navigation and Mapping

AI-driven navigation apps provide real-time traffic updates, suggest faster routes, and offer alternative transportation options. These apps help you make informed decisions about your daily routes, reducing travel time and stress.

Imagine navigating through unfamiliar terrain with confidence, knowing that AI provides you with the best routes and travel options. AI ensures that transportation becomes more convenient and user-friendly.

6. Transportation Accessibility

AI-driven technologies are making transportation more accessible to individuals with disabilities. Self-driving cars, mobility aids, and AI-powered navigation apps can help people with disabilities travel more independently and comfortably.

Imagine a world where everyone has the freedom to travel regardless of their physical limitations, thanks to AI-powered accessibility solutions. AI ensures that transportation becomes more inclusive and equitable.

7. Environmental Sustainability
AI helps reduce the environmental impact of transportation by optimizing fuel efficiency and reducing emissions. Electric vehicles (EVs) benefit from AI-enhanced battery management and energy conservation, making them more sustainable options.
Imagine a future where transportation is not only efficient but also environmentally responsible, contributing to a cleaner planet. AI ensures that transportation becomes more eco-friendly and sustainable.

8. Air Travel Efficiency
AI streamlines air travel operations by optimizing flight routes, reducing delays, and enhancing security. Airports use AI-powered systems for baggage handling, security screening, and passport control, making air travel smoother and more efficient.
Imagine a world where air travel is less prone to delays, security lines move swiftly, and lost luggage is a rare occurrence. AI ensures that air travel becomes more efficient and enjoyable.

9. Personalized Transportation Services
AI can provide personalized transportation services based on your preferences and needs. Ride-sharing apps

can suggest vehicles that accommodate your group size, luggage, or mobility requirements.

Imagine receiving transportation options that are perfectly tailored to your specific needs, ensuring a comfortable and hassle-free journey. AI ensures that transportation becomes more convenient and customized.

10. Predictive Maintenance

AI monitors the condition of vehicles and infrastructure to predict maintenance needs. This reduces the likelihood of breakdowns, enhances safety, and ensures that transportation services are reliable. Imagine a world where you can trust that your vehicle, whether it's a car, bus, or train, is always in optimal condition for your journey. AI ensures that transportation becomes more dependable and trustworthy.

In conclusion, AI-powered transportation is a transformative force that significantly improves your daily life by enhancing safety, efficiency, and convenience in various modes of transport. Whether you're a daily commuter, a traveler, or simply someone who values streamlined

The Perfect Melody: How AI Transforms Your Daily Music Experience

Music is a universal language that has the power to uplift, inspire, and connect us. In today's digital age, Artificial Intelligence (AI) is revolutionizing how we discover and enjoy music. AI-powered personalized music recommendations are significantly enhancing your daily life by tailoring your music listening experience to your unique tastes and preferences. Whether you're a music enthusiast, a casual listener, or someone who enjoys tunes while working or exercising, AI is reshaping the way we experience music. Here's how:

1. Discovering New Favorites

One of the most noticeable ways AI improves your daily life is by helping you discover new music that aligns with your tastes. AI algorithms analyze your listening history, genre preferences, and mood to suggest songs and artists you might enjoy.

Imagine having a constant stream of fresh and exciting music that keeps you engaged and delighted. AI ensures that your music library is a dynamic collection of favorites, both old and new.

2. Personalized Playlists

AI-powered music streaming platforms curate personalized playlists tailored to your mood, activities, and time of day. Whether you're looking for workout tracks, relaxing tunes, or upbeat songs for your morning commute, AI has you covered.

Imagine having the perfect soundtrack for every moment of your day, effortlessly adapting to your needs and enhancing your experiences. AI ensures that your playlists are always in sync with your life.

3. Smarter Radio Stations

AI enhances radio stations by creating personalized stations that cater to your musical preferences. These stations evolve as you explore different genres and artists, ensuring a consistent listening experience.

Imagine tuning in to a radio station that plays your favorite songs, introduces you to new tracks, and never misses a beat when it comes to your musical tastes. AI ensures that radio becomes an even more enjoyable and tailored experience.

4. Recommendations Beyond Your Comfort Zone

AI doesn't just reinforce your existing musical tastes; it also encourages you to explore new genres and artists. It introduces you to music that falls slightly outside your comfort zone, broadening your musical horizons.

Imagine discovering the joy of genres you never thought you'd enjoy, thanks to AI's gentle nudges toward musical exploration. AI ensures that your musical journey becomes more diverse and enriching.

5. Concert and Event Suggestions

AI can inform you about concerts and live events featuring your favorite artists or similar acts. It considers your location and preferences to recommend events you're likely to enjoy, making it easier to catch your favorite artists in action.

Imagine never missing a concert or event that aligns perfectly with your musical tastes and interests. AI ensures that your live music experiences become more tailored and unforgettable.

6. Music for Mood Enhancement

AI analyzes your emotional responses to music and can suggest tracks to match your mood. Whether you need a musical pick-me-up or something soothing to unwind, AI can provide the perfect soundtrack.

Imagine effortlessly finding music that resonates with your emotions, creating a more profound connection with the music you love. AI ensures that your music choices become more attuned to your feelings.

7. Personalized Music Libraries

AI-powered music libraries organize your music collection based on your preferences and listening habits.

They help you find songs quickly and create a more enjoyable and organized listening experience.

Imagine having a music library that feels like it was custom-designed just for you, making it easy to find your favorite tunes. AI ensures that your music collection becomes more user-friendly and intuitive.

8. Cross-Platform Consistency

AI ensures that your personalized music experience is consistent across various platforms and devices. Whether you're listening on your phone, computer, or smart speaker, your music recommendations and playlists remain synchronized.

Imagine seamlessly transitioning between devices without losing your musical context or playlists. AI ensures that your music experience is uninterrupted and hassle-free.

9. Enhanced Music Education

AI can also serve as a music education tool by providing insights into song composition, musical theory, and historical context. It helps you gain a deeper appreciation and understanding of the music you love.

Imagine delving into the intricacies of your favorite songs and gaining a newfound respect for the artists and composers behind them. AI ensures that your music education becomes more engaging and informative.

10. Accessibility and Inclusivity
AI-driven music recommendations can make music more accessible to individuals with disabilities. Voice-controlled music platforms and AI-assisted devices empower everyone to enjoy music, regardless of physical limitations. Imagine a world where everyone can engage with music on their terms, breaking down barriers to accessibility. AI ensures that music becomes more inclusive and universally enjoyed.

In conclusion, AI-powered personalized music recommendations are a transformative force that significantly improves your daily life by tailoring your music listening experience to your unique tastes and preferences. Whether you're seeking new favorites, personalized playlists, or a deeper connection with

The Culinary Revolution: How AI is Transforming Your Everyday Cooking Experience

Food is an integral part of our daily lives, and the integration of Artificial Intelligence (AI) is reshaping how we cook, eat, and savor flavors. AI-powered cooking innovations are significantly enhancing your daily life by offering personalized recipes, streamlining meal preparation, and even assisting with dietary choices. Whether you're an aspiring chef, a busy professional, or simply someone who enjoys delicious home-cooked meals, AI is transforming the way we experience cooking. Here's how:

1. Personalized Recipe Recommendations
One of the most noticeable ways AI improves your daily life is by providing personalized recipe recommendations. AI algorithms analyze your dietary preferences, ingredient availability, and previous cooking history to suggest recipes tailored to your tastes and dietary restrictions.
Imagine having a personal chef who curates recipes just for you, ensuring that every meal you prepare is both enjoyable and suitable for your nutritional needs. AI ensures that your culinary adventures become more personalized and satisfying.

2. Ingredient Substitution
AI can suggest ingredient substitutions based on what you have in your pantry or dietary restrictions. It helps you adapt recipes to accommodate allergies or dietary preferences without compromising on taste.
Imagine confidently preparing a recipe even when you're missing a few ingredients, knowing that AI can recommend suitable substitutes to maintain flavor and

texture. AI ensures that your cooking becomes more adaptable and resourceful.

3. Cooking Assistance and Timers

AI-powered kitchen devices and apps offer cooking assistance and timers that guide you through each step of a recipe. These tools ensure that your dishes are cooked to perfection, even if you're not an experienced chef. Imagine effortlessly preparing restaurant-quality dishes at home, with AI providing precise instructions and reminders for each cooking stage. AI ensures that your culinary skills improve and your meals are consistently delicious.

4. Nutrition Analysis

AI can analyze the nutritional content of recipes and provide information on calorie counts, macronutrients, and vitamins. This helps you make informed dietary choices and maintain a healthy lifestyle.

Imagine being able to evaluate the nutritional value of every meal you prepare, allowing you to make conscious decisions about your diet. AI ensures that your cooking becomes more health-conscious and beneficial.

5. Meal Planning and Grocery Lists

AI-powered meal planning apps can create weekly menus, generate shopping lists, and even suggest recipes based on what ingredients you already have. This streamlines meal preparation and reduces food waste. Imagine having a comprehensive meal plan and a shopping list at your fingertips, making grocery shopping and meal preparation efficient and stress-free. AI ensures that your cooking becomes more organized and sustainable.

6. Culinary Creativity

AI can inspire culinary creativity by offering unique ingredient combinations and flavor profiles. It encourages you to experiment with new tastes and techniques, expanding your culinary repertoire. Imagine exploring a world of flavors and experimenting with ingredients you never thought to pair, all with the guidance and inspiration of AI. AI ensures that your cooking becomes more adventurous and enjoyable.

7. Dietary Guidance

AI can offer dietary guidance and recommendations based on your health goals. Whether you're aiming to lose weight, build muscle, or follow a specific diet plan, AI can provide tailored advice. Imagine having a virtual nutritionist who understands your goals and guides you toward making food choices that align with your objectives. AI ensures that your dietary journey becomes more personalized and effective.

8. International Cuisine Exploration

AI can introduce you to international cuisines by suggesting recipes and guiding you through the preparation of dishes from around the world. You can embark on a culinary journey without leaving your kitchen.

Imagine traveling through your taste buds, exploring the rich and diverse flavors of global cuisine with AI as your culinary tour guide. AI ensures that your cooking becomes more culturally enriching and exciting.

9. Cooking for Dietary Restrictions

AI-powered cooking solutions can help individuals with dietary restrictions, such as allergies or intolerances, by suggesting safe and enjoyable recipes. This ensures that dietary limitations do not limit culinary creativity. Imagine cooking delicious meals that cater to your dietary restrictions, allowing you to savor flavors without worrying about potential allergens. AI ensures that your cooking becomes more accommodating and enjoyable.

10. Culinary Community and Inspiration

AI-powered cooking apps and platforms connect you with a community of fellow food enthusiasts and chefs. You can share recipes, get inspired by others, and exchange culinary experiences. Imagine being part of a vibrant online culinary community where you can learn from others, share your culinary creations, and find inspiration for your next meal. AI ensures that your cooking becomes more social and collaborative.

In conclusion, AI-powered cooking innovations are transforming your daily life by offering personalized recipes, simplifying meal preparation, and assisting with dietary choices. Whether you're a novice cook or a seasoned chef, AI ensures that your culinary journey becomes more enjoyable, efficient, and tailored to your tastes and dietary needs. As AI technology continues to advance, the future of AI in cooking holds the promise of even more personalized, creative, and delightful culinary experiences, enriching your daily life one meal at a time.

Navigating Tomorrow: How AI is Transforming Your Daily Travel Experience

Travel is an essential part of our lives, whether for business, leisure, or daily commuting. In today's digital age, Artificial Intelligence (AI) is revolutionizing how we experience travel. AI-powered travel solutions are significantly enhancing your daily life by making your journeys more convenient, efficient, and personalized. Whether you're a frequent flyer, a daily commuter, or an adventure seeker, AI is reshaping the way we navigate the world. Here's how:

1. Personalized Travel Recommendations
One of the most noticeable ways AI improves your daily life is by providing personalized travel recommendations. AI algorithms analyze your travel history, preferences, and interests to suggest destinations, accommodations, and activities tailored to your taste.
Imagine receiving travel suggestions that align perfectly with your interests, ensuring that every trip you take is a memorable and fulfilling experience. AI ensures that your travel plans become more personalized and enjoyable.

2. Efficient Trip Planning
AI-powered travel platforms can streamline the trip planning process by aggregating information from various sources, such as flights, accommodations, and local attractions. They offer you a consolidated view of your itinerary, making it easier to plan your trips.
Imagine planning your entire trip, from booking flights to finding the best local restaurants, all within a single

platform that adapts to your preferences. AI ensures that trip planning becomes more efficient and stress-free.

3. Real-Time Travel Updates

AI provides real-time travel updates, including flight delays, gate changes, and traffic conditions. These updates keep you informed and help you adjust your plans on the go, reducing travel-related stress.
Imagine having instant access to essential travel information, allowing you to make informed decisions and avoid unnecessary delays or inconveniences. AI ensures that your travel experiences become more seamless and worry-free.

4. Language Translation and Communication

AI-powered translation apps and devices facilitate communication in foreign countries, overcoming language barriers. These tools help you navigate unfamiliar environments, order food, and interact with locals with ease.
Imagine traveling to any corner of the world with the confidence that language differences won't hinder your ability to communicate and immerse yourself in new cultures. AI ensures that travel becomes more accessible and inclusive.

5. Personal Travel Assistants

AI-driven virtual travel assistants can answer your questions, provide recommendations, and assist with booking accommodations and activities. They act as your personalized travel concierge, available 24/7. Imagine having a knowledgeable travel companion by your side throughout your journey, ensuring that your every need is met, no matter where you are in the world. AI ensures that travel becomes more convenient and supported.

6. Predictive Travel Analytics

AI analyzes historical travel data and predicts travel trends. This information can help you find the best times to book flights, secure the most affordable accommodations, and avoid tourist crowds.
Imagine optimizing your travel plans to save money and enjoy destinations during their off-peak seasons, all thanks to AI-driven insights. AI ensures that travel becomes more cost-effective and enjoyable.

7. Enhanced Airport Experiences

AI enhances airport experiences by providing information on security wait times, airport amenities, and even suggesting places to dine or shop based on your preferences and location within the terminal. Imagine navigating airports with ease, knowing exactly where to go and how to make the most of your time between flights. AI ensures that airport experiences become more efficient and enjoyable.

8. Sustainable Travel Options

AI-powered travel platforms can suggest sustainable travel options, such as eco-friendly accommodations and transportation. They help you make more environmentally responsible choices while exploring the world. Imagine traveling with the assurance that your choices align with your commitment to environmental sustainability, helping to reduce your carbon footprint. AI ensures that travel becomes more eco-conscious and responsible.

9. Personalized Travel Insurance

AI can recommend personalized travel insurance plans based on your itinerary, medical history, and travel activities. This ensures that you have the right coverage for your specific needs and circumstances. Imagine having travel insurance that's tailored to your trip, providing you with peace of mind and financial protection in case of unexpected events. AI ensures that travel insurance becomes more customized and comprehensive.

10. Accessible Travel for All

AI-powered travel solutions are making travel more accessible to individuals with disabilities. They provide information on accessible accommodations, transportation, and attractions, ensuring that everyone can explore the world. Imagine a world where travel is truly inclusive, allowing people of all abilities to embark on unforgettable journeys. AI ensures that travel becomes more accessible and diverse.

In conclusion, AI-powered travel solutions are a transformative force that significantly improves your daily life by making your journeys more convenient, efficient, and personalized. Whether you're a seasoned traveler or someone looking to explore new horizons, AI ensures that travel becomes more enjoyable, accessible, and tailored to your preferences and needs. As AI technology continues to advance, the future of AI in travel holds the promise of even more seamless, sustainable, and enriching travel experiences, turning your wanderlust dreams into reality.

Bridging the World: How AI Transforms Your Daily Life Through Language Translation

In our increasingly interconnected world, language can sometimes be a barrier to communication and understanding. Enter Artificial Intelligence (AI), which is revolutionizing language translation and significantly enhancing your daily life. AI-powered translation tools are making communication across languages more accessible, efficient, and accurate. Whether you're traveling, working globally, or simply seeking to connect with people from diverse linguistic backgrounds, AI is reshaping the way we break down language barriers. Here's how:

1. Instant Translation on the Go
One of the most noticeable ways AI improves your daily life is through instant translation on your mobile devices. AI-powered translation apps enable you to communicate in real-time with people who speak different languages. Whether you're asking for directions in a foreign city or having a business meeting with international partners, AI can help bridge the language gap.
Imagine exploring the world with the confidence that you can communicate effectively, no matter where you are. AI ensures that your travels become more immersive and less reliant on language proficiency.

2. Accurate Business Communication
AI enhances business communication by providing precise and reliable translations for emails, documents, and presentations. It ensures that your professional correspondence maintains its intended meaning, even when dealing with clients or colleagues from diverse linguistic backgrounds.

Imagine conducting international business seamlessly, knowing that AI is there to assist you in conveying your message accurately and professionally. AI ensures that your work becomes more efficient and globally competitive.

3. Multilingual Content Creation

AI enables content creators to reach broader audiences by translating their work into multiple languages. It expands the reach of your blog, website, or social media content, allowing you to connect with people from around the world. Imagine sharing your ideas and creativity with a global audience, knowing that AI can help you translate your content with precision and fluency. AI ensures that your content becomes more inclusive and far-reaching.

4. Access to Multilingual Education

AI-powered language translation tools make educational content from around the world more accessible. Whether you're learning a new language or exploring academic resources, AI can provide translations and explanations to aid your comprehension.

5. Enhanced Cultural Exchange

AI fosters cultural exchange by facilitating conversations and interactions between people from different cultures.

It encourages cross-cultural understanding and promotes friendships and connections beyond language barriers. Imagine connecting with individuals from diverse backgrounds and learning about their cultures and perspectives, all thanks to AI-powered translation tools. AI ensures that your social interactions become more inclusive and enlightening.

6. Preservation of Indigenous Languages
AI plays a role in preserving endangered languages by providing translation and transcription services. It aids in documenting and revitalizing indigenous languages that are at risk of fading away.
Imagine contributing to the preservation of linguistic diversity and cultural heritage by using AI to document and promote indigenous languages. AI ensures that language preservation efforts become more effective and meaningful.

7. Reliable Travel Experiences
AI-powered translation tools can translate signs, menus, and instructions in foreign countries, making your travel experiences more enjoyable and less confusing. Whether you're dining at a local restaurant or navigating public transportation, AI helps you feel more at ease in unfamiliar surroundings.
Imagine traveling with the assurance that you can read and understand essential information, enhancing your

sense of adventure and exploration. AI ensures that your travel experiences become more immersive and worry-free.

8. Inclusive Customer Support

AI-driven chatbots and customer support services can offer multilingual assistance, ensuring that customers from different linguistic backgrounds receive support in their preferred language. This makes businesses more accessible and customer-focused.

Imagine interacting with customer support that understands your language and provides efficient assistance, regardless of where you're located. AI ensures that customer support becomes more inclusive and responsive.

9. Faster Language Learning

AI can accelerate language learning by providing instant translations and explanations. Language learners can practice listening, speaking, and reading in their target language with the help of AI-powered language tools. Imagine learning a new language with greater efficiency and effectiveness, thanks to AI-guided practice and real-time feedback. AI ensures that language learning becomes more engaging and accessible.

10. Bridging Humanitarian Efforts

AI-powered translation tools can be instrumental in humanitarian efforts, facilitating communication with refugees, migrants, and people affected by natural disasters. They ensure that aid workers and volunteers can effectively communicate and provide assistance. Imagine being part of humanitarian efforts that transcend language barriers, enabling relief and support to reach those in need more efficiently. AI ensures that humanitarian initiatives become more impactful and inclusive.

In conclusion, AI-powered language translation is a transformative force that significantly improves your daily life by breaking down language barriers and fostering global communication. Whether you're traveling, working, learning, or connecting with people from diverse backgrounds, AI ensures that language is no longer a hindrance to understanding and collaboration. As AI technology continues to advance, the future of AI in language translation holds the promise of even more accurate, efficient, and culturally sensitive communication, bringing people and cultures closer together in a world without linguistic boundaries.

Transforming Justice: How AI Revolutionizes Your Daily Life Through Legal Services

The legal field, with its complexities and intricacies, has long been considered a realm untouched by technology. However, in recent years, Artificial Intelligence (AI) has emerged as a transformative force in legal services, significantly enhancing your daily life by improving access to justice, streamlining legal processes, and making legal information more readily available. Whether you're dealing with a legal issue, seeking legal advice, or simply interested in understanding your rights, AI is reshaping the way we navigate the legal world. Here's how:

1. Legal Research and Information Retrieval
One of the most noticeable ways AI improves your daily life is by making legal research and information retrieval more efficient. AI-powered legal research tools can analyze vast databases of case law, statutes, and regulations to provide accurate and relevant legal information in a fraction of the time it would take a human researcher.
Imagine having access to a comprehensive legal library at your fingertips, enabling you to quickly find answers to legal questions, understand your rights, and make

informed decisions. AI ensures that legal information becomes more accessible and user-friendly.

2. Virtual Legal Assistants

AI-driven virtual legal assistants can help you draft legal documents, such as contracts, wills, and agreements, with ease. These virtual assistants guide you through the document creation process, ensuring that your documents are accurate and legally sound.
Imagine being able to create legally binding documents without the need for expensive legal consultations, saving both time and money. AI ensures that legal document preparation becomes more accessible and affordable.

3. Predictive Analytics

AI can analyze legal data to predict case outcomes and assess the likelihood of success in legal matters. This technology helps lawyers and individuals make informed decisions about pursuing legal actions, settling disputes, or negotiating settlements.
Imagine having insights into the potential outcomes of your legal case, allowing you to make strategic decisions that maximize your chances of success. AI ensures that legal strategy becomes more data-driven and effective.

4. Automated Legal Processes

AI automates repetitive and time-consuming legal processes, such as contract review and due diligence. It streamlines the legal workflow, reducing the need for manual labor and increasing efficiency in legal practice. Imagine legal professionals being able to focus on high-value tasks and providing more personalized service to clients, thanks to AI handling routine tasks. AI ensures that legal processes become more efficient and cost-effective.

5. Legal Aid and Access to Justice
AI-powered chatbots and virtual legal assistants can provide legal information and guidance to individuals who cannot afford legal representation. This technology expands access to justice and ensures that everyone can understand their rights and navigate legal issues. Imagine marginalized and underserved communities having access to legal assistance and information, promoting fairness and equality in the legal system. AI ensures that access to justice becomes more inclusive and equitable.

6. Regulatory Compliance
AI can help businesses and organizations stay compliant with ever-changing regulations and legal requirements. It monitors regulatory updates and provides guidance on compliance measures, reducing the risk of legal violations.

Imagine businesses operating confidently, knowing that AI helps them navigate complex legal regulations and avoid costly legal disputes. AI ensures that regulatory compliance becomes more manageable and proactive.

7. Legal Search Engines

AI-powered legal search engines provide accurate and relevant search results for legal queries. These engines help lawyers, legal researchers, and individuals find specific cases, statutes, and legal opinions quickly and efficiently.

Imagine being able to find the precise legal information you need within seconds, simplifying the legal research process and reducing the risk of overlooking critical details. AI ensures that legal search becomes more precise and time-saving.

8. Language Translation in Legal Documents

AI assists in translating legal documents from one language to another while preserving the legal accuracy and integrity of the content. This ensures that legal agreements are accessible to individuals and businesses operating globally.

Imagine conducting international business with confidence, knowing that AI can accurately translate legal documents, preventing misunderstandings and legal disputes due to language barriers. AI ensures that legal language translation becomes more reliable and inclusive.

9. Reduced Legal Costs

AI-driven legal services often come at a lower cost than traditional legal consultations. This affordability allows individuals and small businesses to access legal assistance and representation that might have been financially out of reach in the past.

Imagine having access to legal support without the burden of exorbitant legal fees, making it easier to resolve legal issues and protect your rights. AI ensures that legal services become more affordable and accessible to a broader audience.

10. Enhanced Legal Data Security

AI can bolster legal data security by identifying potential vulnerabilities and threats in legal systems. It helps protect sensitive legal information from breaches and cyberattacks, safeguarding the confidentiality of legal matters.

Imagine your legal documents and sensitive information being stored and transmitted with the highest level of security, ensuring the privacy and integrity of your legal affairs. AI ensures that legal data security becomes more robust and dependable.

In conclusion, AI-powered legal services are a transformative force that significantly improves your daily life by enhancing access to justice, streamlining legal processes, and making legal information more accessible. Whether you're seeking legal advice, navigating a legal dispute, or simply interested in understanding your rights, AI ensures that the legal world becomes more user-friendly, efficient, and equitable. As AI technology continues to advance, the future of AI in legal services holds the promise of even more accessible, efficient, and accurate legal support, empowering individuals and businesses to navigate the complexities of the legal landscape with confidence and ease.

Amplifying Your Daily Commute: How AI is Revolutionizing Podcasts

Podcasts have become an integral part of modern life, offering an endless stream of knowledge, entertainment, and inspiration. Now, Artificial Intelligence (AI) is ushering in a new era for podcasting, enhancing your daily life by making content more personalized, discoverable, and engaging. Whether you're a podcast enthusiast, a casual listener, or someone looking to make the most of your commute or workout, AI is reshaping the way we experience audio content.

1. Personalized Content Recommendations
One of the most noticeable ways AI improves your daily life is by providing personalized podcast recommendations. AI algorithms analyze your listening history, interests, and preferences to suggest podcasts that align with your tastes.
Imagine having a curated playlist of podcasts that caters to your specific interests and keeps you engaged and informed during your daily commute. AI ensures that your podcasting experience becomes more tailored and enjoyable.

2. Content Discovery
AI-powered podcast platforms use natural language processing and machine learning to understand the content of podcasts. They can recommend episodes based on specific topics, keywords, or even your mood. Imagine easily discovering podcasts that match your current interests or curiosity, allowing you to dive into topics that resonate with you on any given day. AI ensures that content discovery becomes more intuitive and responsive to your needs.

3. Transcription and Search

AI can transcribe podcast episodes into text, making them searchable. You can quickly find specific information or quotes from your favorite podcasts by using keywords or phrases.

Imagine being able to reference valuable information from podcasts as easily as you search for information on the web. AI ensures that podcasts become more accessible and research-friendly.

4. Automated Translations

AI-driven language translation tools can translate podcasts into different languages in real-time. This allows you to access content from around the world, breaking down language barriers.

Imagine enjoying podcasts in languages you don't speak fluently, broadening your cultural horizons and learning from global perspectives. AI ensures that podcasts become more inclusive and internationally accessible.

5. Voice Assistant Integration

AI-powered voice assistants like Siri, Google Assistant, and Alexa can help you discover and play podcasts using voice commands. You can ask your device to find podcasts on specific topics or from your favorite creators.

Imagine having hands-free control over your podcast listening experience, making it safer and more convenient while driving or doing household chores. AI ensures that podcasts become more integrated into your daily routines.

6. Podcast Creation Assistance

AI can assist podcast creators by automating tasks like audio editing, background noise reduction, and transcript generation. This simplifies the podcast production process, allowing creators to focus on content.
Imagine podcasters being able to create high-quality content more efficiently, resulting in a wider variety of engaging podcasts for you to enjoy. AI ensures that the podcasting landscape becomes more diverse and creative.

7. Ad Targeting and Personalization

AI helps podcast advertisers target their ads more effectively. It analyzes listener data to deliver ads that are relevant to your interests, reducing irrelevant and intrusive advertising.
Imagine hearing ads that align with your interests, making the advertising experience more engaging and less disruptive. AI ensures that podcast ads become more personalized and enjoyable.

8. Accessibility Features

AI enhances podcast accessibility for individuals with disabilities. It can provide audio descriptions of visual content, transcribe episodes for those with hearing impairments, and offer navigation assistance for screen readers.

Imagine everyone, regardless of their abilities, being able to enjoy and benefit from the wealth of content available in the podcasting world. AI ensures that podcasts become more inclusive and accessible to all.

9. Data-Driven Content Improvement

AI analyzes listener data and feedback to help podcast creators understand their audience better. This insight allows them to refine their content and delivery to better meet the needs and preferences of their listeners. Imagine podcasts continually improving to provide you with more engaging and valuable content that resonates with your interests. AI ensures that podcast creators become more responsive to audience feedback.

10. Enhanced User Experience

AI-powered podcast apps can learn your listening habits and preferences over time, fine-tuning the content they recommend to you. This results in a more enjoyable and user-friendly experience.

Imagine a podcast app that gets better at serving you the content you love the more you use it, ensuring that your podcasting experience is continually enriched. AI ensures that podcast apps become more intuitive and user-centered.

In conclusion, AI-powered podcasting is a transformative force that significantly improves your daily life by making audio content more personalized, discoverable, and engaging. Whether you're seeking information, entertainment, or inspiration, AI ensures that podcasts become a richer and more accessible source of knowledge and enjoyment. As AI technology continues to advance, the future of AI in podcasting holds the promise of even more tailored, diverse, and immersive audio experiences, turning your daily routines into opportunities for learning and discovery through the power of audio.

Spotless Living: How AI is Revolutionizing Home Cleaning

Home cleaning has always been a chore that demands time and effort. However, in recent years, Artificial Intelligence (AI) has emerged as a game-changer in home cleaning, making your daily life more convenient, efficient, and enjoyable. AI-powered cleaning devices and technologies are transforming the way you maintain your living spaces. Whether you're a busy professional, a parent juggling multiple responsibilities, or simply someone who values a clean home, AI is reshaping the way we keep our surroundings spotless. Here's how:

1. Smart Vacuum Cleaners

One of the most noticeable ways AI improves your daily life is through smart vacuum cleaners. These devices use AI algorithms to navigate your home, avoiding obstacles and efficiently covering every area. They can be controlled remotely through your smartphone or integrated into your smart home system.

Imagine coming home to a clean and dust-free environment without having to lift a finger. AI ensures that your home cleaning becomes more hands-free and time-saving.

2. Precision Cleaning

AI-powered cleaning robots use sensors and cameras to detect dirt and grime in real-time. They focus on areas that need the most attention, ensuring a more thorough and efficient cleaning process.

Imagine having a cleaning assistant that doesn't miss a spot and is always ready to tackle the dirtiest areas of your home. AI ensures that your cleaning becomes more precise and effective.

3. Voice-Activated Cleaning

Some AI-enabled cleaning devices can be controlled through voice commands, making it even more convenient to start cleaning tasks. You can simply ask your AI assistant to schedule cleaning sessions or spot clean specific areas.

Imagine directing your cleaning robot with a simple voice command, allowing you to multitask or relax while your home gets cleaned. AI ensures that home cleaning becomes more effortless and integrated into your daily routines.

4. Customized Cleaning Schedules

AI-powered cleaning devices can learn your cleaning preferences and create customized cleaning schedules. They adapt to your lifestyle, ensuring that your home is cleaned at the times that suit you best.

Imagine a cleaning schedule that aligns with your daily routines, making it easy to maintain a consistently clean home. AI ensures that your cleaning becomes more tailored to your needs.

5. Allergy and Air Quality Control

Some AI-driven cleaning devices are equipped with air quality sensors that detect allergens and pollutants. They can adjust their cleaning intensity based on the air quality, ensuring a healthier living environment.

Imagine breathing cleaner air and experiencing fewer allergy symptoms, thanks to AI-powered cleaning devices that prioritize air quality. AI ensures that your home cleaning becomes more health-conscious and beneficial.

6. Smart Mopping Systems

AI-driven mopping robots can detect different floor types and adjust their cleaning methods accordingly. They can also avoid carpets and rugs to prevent unnecessary dampening.

Imagine having sparkling clean floors without the hassle of manual mopping, and without worrying about damaging your carpets. AI ensures that your floor cleaning becomes more efficient and hassle-free.

7. Maintenance Alerts

AI-enabled cleaning devices can send maintenance alerts when it's time to replace filters or brushes. This ensures that your cleaning appliances continue to work effectively and prolongs their lifespan.

Imagine never missing a critical maintenance task and always having your cleaning devices in optimal working condition. AI ensures that your cleaning becomes more reliable and cost-effective.

8. Reduced Energy Consumption

AI-powered cleaning devices are designed to be energy-efficient. They can optimize their cleaning routes and adjust their power settings to conserve energy while still delivering effective cleaning results.

Imagine enjoying a clean home without significantly impacting your energy bills, thanks to AI's energy-conscious cleaning technology. AI ensures that your cleaning becomes more eco-friendly and cost-efficient.

9. Enhanced Home Security
Some AI-enabled cleaning robots can also function as home security devices. They can patrol your home, detect unusual movements, and even send alerts to your smartphone if something is amiss.
Imagine having an extra layer of security for your home while your cleaning robot goes about its tasks. AI ensures that your cleaning becomes more integrated with your home's safety.

10. Time and Stress Savings
Perhaps the most significant benefit of AI in home cleaning is the time and stress it saves. You no longer need to spend hours on cleaning tasks, allowing you to focus on other aspects of your life and enjoy a cleaner home without the hassle.

In conclusion, AI-powered home cleaning is a transformative force that significantly improves your daily life by making home maintenance more convenient, efficient, and enjoyable. Whether you have a busy schedule or simply want to simplify your cleaning routine, AI ensures that your living spaces remain spotless without the stress and time commitment. As AI technology continues to advance, the future of AI in home cleaning holds the promise of even more intelligent, adaptable, and user-friendly cleaning solutions, allowing you to enjoy the benefits of a cleaner home with greater ease and comfort.

Elevating Entertainment: How AI Transforms Your Daily Enjoyment

Entertainment has always been an integral part of our lives, offering a much-needed escape from the daily grind and a source of joy and inspiration. Now, Artificial Intelligence (AI) is revolutionizing the world of entertainment, making your daily life more engaging, immersive, and personalized. AI-powered technologies are redefining the way we consume and interact with entertainment content. Whether you're a movie buff, a music lover, a gamer, or someone seeking new forms of amusement, AI is reshaping the way we experience entertainment. Here's how:

1. Personalized Content Recommendations
One of the most noticeable ways AI improves your daily life is through personalized content recommendations. AI algorithms analyze your viewing, listening, or gaming habits and preferences to suggest content tailored to your taste.

Imagine having a streaming service that always knows what you want to watch or listen to next, ensuring that your entertainment experiences remain engaging and relevant. AI ensures that your entertainment choices become more tailored and enjoyable.

2. Content Discovery

AI-powered platforms use natural language processing and machine learning to understand content in movies, music, books, and more. This enables them to recommend entertainment options based on specific topics, themes, or even your current mood.
Imagine effortlessly discovering new movies, music, or books that align with your current interests, making your entertainment choices more diverse and exciting. AI ensures that content discovery becomes more intuitive and responsive to your preferences.

3. Personalized Soundtracks

AI can create personalized soundtracks for your life by analyzing your daily activities, emotions, and preferences. It can curate playlists or music suggestions that match your mood, whether you're working out, relaxing, or celebrating a special occasion.
Imagine having a music playlist that perfectly complements every moment of your day, enhancing your experiences and setting the right mood. AI ensures that

your music enjoyment becomes more tailored and immersive.

4. Interactive Storytelling
AI is changing the way stories are told in video games and interactive media. AI-driven characters can adapt their behavior and dialogue based on your choices, creating a dynamic and personalized narrative experience.
Imagine playing a video game where your decisions truly shape the outcome of the story, making each playthrough a unique and immersive adventure. AI ensures that interactive storytelling becomes more engaging and replayable.

5. Personalized Movie and TV Show Recuts
AI can analyze movies and TV shows to create personalized recuts that focus on your favorite characters, storylines, or moments. This allows you to rewatch your favorite content in a new and exciting way. Imagine watching your favorite movie or TV show from a fresh perspective, highlighting the aspects that matter most to you. AI ensures that your entertainment experiences become more personalized and enjoyable.

6. Language Translation in Entertainment
AI-driven language translation tools can provide subtitles and dubbing for movies, TV shows, and video

games in multiple languages. This enables you to enjoy content from around the world without language barriers. Imagine watching foreign films or playing international video games with subtitles or voiceovers that capture the essence of the original content. AI ensures that language doesn't limit your entertainment choices.

7. AI-Enhanced Visual Effects

AI is improving the quality of visual effects in movies and games. It can enhance graphics, create realistic animations, and even generate entire virtual worlds, making entertainment experiences more visually stunning and immersive.

Imagine watching a movie or playing a game with breathtaking visuals that rival the quality of Hollywood blockbusters. AI ensures that visual effects in entertainment become more impressive and captivating.

8. AI-Generated Art and Music

AI algorithms can create original art and music, opening up new possibilities for creativity and expression. AI-generated content can be used in various forms of entertainment, from music composition to visual art in video games.

Imagine experiencing art and music that push the boundaries of creativity and challenge traditional notions of what's possible. AI ensures that artistic expression in entertainment becomes more innovative and limitless.

9. Realistic Animation and Virtual Characters
AI-driven animation technologies create more lifelike and expressive characters in movies and video games. These characters can convey emotions and interact with players or viewers in more convincing ways.
Imagine watching a movie or playing a game where characters feel like real individuals with their own thoughts and emotions, deepening your connection to the story. AI ensures that virtual characters become more relatable and engaging.

10. Enhanced User Experiences
AI can analyze user behavior and feedback to improve the overall entertainment experience. It can optimize streaming quality, suggest content improvements, and provide faster customer support for any issues.

In conclusion, AI-powered entertainment is a transformative force that significantly improves your daily life by making entertainment more engaging, immersive, and personalized. Whether you're watching a movie, listening to music, playing a game, or seeking artistic inspiration, AI ensures that your entertainment experiences become more captivating and tailored to your preferences. As AI technology continues to advance, the future of AI in entertainment holds the promise of even more innovative, interactive, and emotionally resonant forms of entertainment, turning every moment of leisure into an opportunity for exploration and enjoyment.

Energizing Your Everyday: How AI Transforms Your Daily Life Through Energy Management

Energy management is a critical aspect of modern life, affecting everything from your electricity bills to your environmental footprint. In recent years, Artificial Intelligence (AI) has emerged as a powerful tool for optimizing energy use, making your daily life more efficient, cost-effective, and sustainable. AI-driven technologies are reshaping the way we consume and manage energy. Whether you're looking to reduce your utility bills, minimize your environmental impact, or simply ensure a more reliable energy supply, AI is revolutionizing the way we interact with energy.

1. Smart Home Energy Efficiency
One of the most noticeable ways AI improves your daily life is through smart home energy efficiency systems. AI algorithms analyze your energy consumption patterns and adjust heating, cooling, and lighting systems to

optimize energy use. These systems can also learn your preferences and adjust settings accordingly.

Imagine coming home to a perfectly comfortable environment that's energy-efficient and tailored to your preferences, without the need for manual adjustments. AI ensures that your home becomes more energy-efficient and comfortable.

2. Predictive Energy Management

AI can predict your energy usage patterns based on historical data, weather forecasts, and other factors. This enables it to optimize your energy consumption, ensuring that you use energy when it's most cost-effective and efficient.

Imagine reducing your energy bills by optimizing energy use during off-peak hours and avoiding energy-intensive activities during peak times. AI ensures that your energy management becomes more cost-effective and sustainable.

3. Renewable Energy Integration

AI can optimize the use of renewable energy sources like solar panels and wind turbines by predicting when these sources will generate the most power. It can also manage energy storage systems to store excess energy for use during cloudy or windless periods.

Imagine harnessing the full potential of renewable energy sources to power your home and reduce your reliance on fossil fuels. AI ensures that renewable energy integration becomes more efficient and reliable.

4. Energy Consumption Insights

AI-driven energy management systems provide real-time insights into your energy consumption. You can monitor which devices consume the most energy and make informed decisions to reduce energy waste.

Imagine having a clear understanding of your energy usage habits and being able to take steps to reduce waste and lower your energy bills. AI ensures that your energy consumption becomes more transparent and controllable.

5. Demand Response

AI can participate in demand response programs, where it adjusts your energy use in response to grid conditions or price signals. This not only helps balance the energy grid but also allows you to save money during peak pricing hours.

Imagine automatically reducing your energy consumption during high-demand periods and receiving incentives for your contribution to grid stability. AI ensures that demand response becomes more financially rewarding and grid-friendly.

6. Energy-Efficient Appliances

AI-driven appliances and devices are designed to optimize their energy use. For example, smart thermostats can learn your heating and cooling preferences, ensuring that your home stays comfortable while minimizing energy waste.

Imagine having appliances that adapt to your lifestyle, reducing energy consumption without sacrificing comfort or convenience. AI ensures that energy-efficient appliances become more accessible and effective.

7. Grid Management

AI plays a crucial role in managing energy grids efficiently. It can predict and prevent grid failures, balance supply and demand, and optimize the distribution of electricity to reduce losses.

Imagine enjoying a more reliable energy supply with fewer disruptions and blackouts, thanks to AI's grid management capabilities. AI ensures that energy grids become more resilient and efficient.

8. Energy Cost Optimization

AI algorithms can analyze energy prices and consumption patterns to help you choose the best energy plans and providers. This ensures that you get the most cost-effective energy supply for your needs.

Imagine lowering your energy bills by selecting the most economical energy plans and optimizing your consumption accordingly. AI ensures that energy cost optimization becomes more accessible and beneficial.

9. Environmental Impact Reduction

AI helps reduce your environmental footprint by optimizing energy use and promoting the adoption of renewable energy sources. It calculates and visualizes the environmental impact of your energy consumption, encouraging more sustainable choices.

Imagine knowing the environmental impact of your energy usage and taking steps to reduce your carbon footprint by using clean energy sources. AI ensures that your energy consumption becomes more eco-conscious and responsible.

10. Emergency Response

AI can enhance energy management during emergencies by identifying critical infrastructure and prioritizing energy distribution to essential facilities like hospitals and emergency shelters. It ensures a more resilient response to crises.

Imagine having a more reliable energy supply during emergencies, ensuring that critical services remain operational when they are needed most. AI ensures that emergency response becomes more effective and responsive.

In conclusion, AI-powered energy management is a transformative force that significantly improves your daily life by making energy use more efficient, cost-effective, and sustainable. Whether you're looking to save money on your utility bills, reduce your environmental impact, or ensure a more reliable energy supply, AI ensures that energy management becomes a more intelligent and accessible endeavor. As AI technology continues to advance, the future of AI in energy management holds the promise of even smarter, more adaptive, and more environmentally friendly solutions, allowing individuals and communities to embrace a greener and more efficient energy future.

Empowering Futures: How AI Transforms Children's Education in Daily Life

Education is the cornerstone of personal and societal growth, and in today's digital age, Artificial Intelligence (AI) is revolutionizing the way children learn and engage with educational content. AI-driven technologies are making education more personalized, interactive, and accessible, significantly enhancing your child's daily life and educational journey. Whether your child is in elementary school, middle school, or high school, AI is reshaping the way we approach education and prepare the next generation for success. Here's how:

1. Personalized Learning Paths

One of the most noticeable ways AI improves children's daily lives is by offering personalized learning paths. AI algorithms analyze a child's strengths, weaknesses, and learning style to tailor educational content accordingly. Imagine your child receiving customized lessons that cater to their specific needs, ensuring that they grasp concepts more effectively and progress at their own pace. AI ensures that learning becomes more individualized and engaging.

2. Adaptive Assessments

AI-powered assessments can adapt to a child's skill level and comprehension. These assessments continuously monitor progress, adjusting the difficulty of questions to challenge students appropriately.

Imagine your child taking tests that evolve in real-time to match their knowledge and abilities, providing more accurate insights into their academic performance. AI ensures that assessments become more informative and constructive.

3. Intelligent Tutoring

AI-driven virtual tutors provide on-demand assistance to children when they're struggling with a concept or question. These virtual tutors can offer explanations, answer questions, and provide additional practice problems.

Imagine your child having access to a patient and knowledgeable tutor at any time, boosting their confidence and comprehension. AI ensures that tutoring becomes more accessible and readily available.

4. Gamified Learning

AI can gamify educational content, turning lessons into interactive and engaging experiences. Gamified learning apps and platforms motivate children to learn through challenges, rewards, and competition.

Imagine your child eagerly diving into educational games that make learning enjoyable and addictive, fostering a love for learning from an early age. AI ensures that learning becomes more fun and immersive.

5. Language Learning

AI-powered language learning apps and platforms offer immersive language acquisition experiences. They use speech recognition and interactive exercises to help children develop language skills naturally.

Imagine your child becoming fluent in a foreign language through interactive lessons that adapt to their progress and pronunciation. AI ensures that language learning becomes more effective and enjoyable.

6. Personalized Feedback

AI can provide instant feedback on assignments and homework, highlighting areas where children excel and areas where they need improvement. This immediate feedback encourages iterative learning.

Imagine your child receiving constructive feedback that helps them refine their skills and understand their strengths and weaknesses better. AI ensures that feedback becomes more valuable and actionable.

7. Enhanced Accessibility

AI-driven educational tools and platforms are designed to be accessible to children with diverse learning needs. They can provide support for students with disabilities, ensuring that no child is left behind.

Imagine all children having equal access to quality education, regardless of their individual learning challenges or abilities. AI ensures that education becomes more inclusive and equitable.

8. Early Intervention

AI can identify early signs of learning difficulties or behavioral issues, allowing for timely intervention and support. It helps educators and parents address potential challenges proactively.

Imagine your child receiving the support they need when facing academic or behavioral challenges, setting them up for future success. AI ensures that early intervention becomes more effective and caring.

9. Remote Learning Support

AI-powered virtual classrooms and educational tools have become essential during times of remote learning, providing children with continuity in their education. Imagine your child seamlessly transitioning to online learning with the help of AI-driven platforms that keep them engaged and connected with their teachers and peers. AI ensures that remote learning becomes more effective and accessible.

10. Education for All

AI-driven educational content can be translated into multiple languages and adapted to various cultural contexts, making quality education more accessible to children around the world. Imagine children from diverse backgrounds having access to high-quality educational resources that reflect their culture and language. AI ensures that education becomes more global and inclusive.

In conclusion, AI-powered education for children is a transformative force that significantly improves their daily lives by making learning more personalized, interactive, and accessible. Whether your child is in a traditional classroom or navigating remote learning, AI ensures that education becomes a dynamic and engaging journey. As AI technology continues to advance, the future of AI in children's education holds the promise of even more intelligent, adaptable, and inclusive learning solutions, empowering the next generation to thrive in an ever-changing world and fostering a lifelong love for learning.

Navigating the Digital Age: How AI Ethics and Awareness Enhance Your Daily Life

In our increasingly digitized world, Artificial Intelligence (AI) plays a prominent role in shaping our daily experiences. Beyond convenience and efficiency, AI ethics and awareness are essential components that ensure the responsible and ethical use of these technologies. By addressing issues of fairness, transparency, and accountability, AI enhances your daily life by promoting ethical behavior in both AI systems and the individuals who create and use them. Here's how AI ethics and awareness contribute to a better daily life:

1. Fair Decision-Making
One of the most noticeable ways AI improves your daily life is by promoting fair decision-making. AI systems, when designed ethically, reduce biases that can

perpetuate discrimination in areas such as hiring, lending, and law enforcement.

Imagine a world where AI systems make decisions based solely on relevant criteria, ensuring fairness and equal opportunities for all individuals, regardless of their background. AI ethics ensures that decision-making becomes more equitable and just.

2. Privacy Protection

AI ethics and awareness emphasize the importance of privacy protection. AI systems must be designed to safeguard your personal data and ensure that it's used responsibly and transparently.

Imagine feeling confident that your data is secure and that AI applications respect your privacy, allowing you to engage with technology without concerns about unauthorized data collection or misuse. AI ethics ensures that your personal information remains protected and respected.

3. Bias Mitigation

AI ethics encourages developers to mitigate bias in AI algorithms and data sets. It promotes fairness in AI systems to prevent them from reinforcing existing societal biases.

Imagine interacting with AI systems that treat everyone equally and fairly, regardless of their race, gender, or other characteristics. AI ethics ensures that AI becomes a tool for promoting diversity and inclusion.

4. Transparency and Accountability

AI ethics emphasizes the importance of transparency in AI systems. It encourages organizations to provide clear explanations of how AI decisions are made and promotes accountability for any harm caused by AI.
Imagine knowing how AI systems arrive at their conclusions and being able to hold organizations responsible for any ethical violations. AI ethics ensures that AI becomes more transparent and accountable.

5. Improved Safety

AI awareness leads to the development of safety measures in AI technologies, such as autonomous vehicles and medical diagnostics. Ethical considerations prioritize the safety of individuals when AI systems are deployed.
Imagine using self-driving cars and medical diagnosis tools that prioritize your safety, reducing the risk of accidents or misdiagnoses. AI ethics ensures that AI technologies become safer and more reliable.

6. Informed Consent

AI ethics underscores the importance of informed consent when collecting and using personal data. It

empowers individuals to make informed decisions about how their data is used.
Imagine having control over how your data is shared and used in AI applications, allowing you to protect your privacy and maintain autonomy over your information.
AI ethics ensures that
informed consent becomes a fundamental principle in AI interactions.

7. Enhanced Consumer Trust
AI ethics and awareness contribute to building and maintaining consumer trust. When individuals believe that AI systems are designed and used ethically, they are more likely to embrace and benefit from AI technologies.
Imagine feeling confident in using AI-driven products and services because you trust that they adhere to ethical principles and prioritize your well-being. AI ethics ensures that consumer trust in AI becomes stronger and more enduring.

8. Ethical AI Development
AI ethics encourages organizations and developers to prioritize ethics in the development process. This includes considering the ethical implications of AI from the outset and continuously monitoring and updating AI systems to ensure ethical behavior.

Imagine AI systems that are continually audited and improved to ensure they meet ethical standards, resulting in more responsible and reliable technologies. AI ethics ensures that AI development becomes more ethical and accountable.

9. Social Responsibility
AI ethics extends to the broader societal impact of AI technologies. It encourages organizations and individuals to consider the implications of AI on society, including its effects on employment, culture, and education. Imagine a world where AI technologies are developed and used in ways that benefit society as a whole, fostering positive social change and equitable access to AI benefits. AI ethics ensures that AI becomes a force for social responsibility and progress.

10. Empowering Individuals
AI ethics and awareness empower individuals to advocate for ethical AI use and demand transparency and accountability from organizations and governments. It allows individuals to actively participate in shaping the ethical landscape of AI. Imagine having the knowledge and tools to hold organizations and policymakers accountable for ethical AI practices, ensuring that AI is used responsibly and ethically. AI ethics ensures that individuals become advocates for ethical AI use and awareness.

In conclusion, AI ethics and awareness are essential components of the digital age, significantly improving your daily life by promoting ethical behavior in AI systems and fostering responsible AI use. Whether you're interacting with AI-driven technologies at work, at home, or in society, AI ethics ensures that AI becomes a tool for positive change and societal advancement. As AI technology continues to advance, the future of AI ethics and awareness holds the promise of even greater transparency, accountability, and ethical behavior in the world of AI, empowering individuals and society to embrace AI with confidence and trust.